John Milton's
PARADISE LOST

AND OTHER WORKS

MARIAN SELDIN BURKHART
ASSISTANT PROFESSOR OF ENGLISH
STATE UNIVERSITY OF NEW YORK

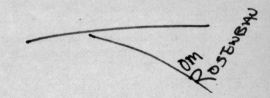

MONARCH PRESS

Published by
MONARCH PRESS
A Simon & Schuster division of
Gulf & Western Corporation
Simon & Schuster Building
1230 Avenue of the Americas
New York, N.Y. 10020

Manufactured in the United States of America

Printed and Bound by Semline, Inc.

1 2 3 4 5 6 7 8 9 10

ISBN: 0-671-00513-8

Library of Congress Catalog Card Number: 66-29376

CONTENTS

INTRODUCTION

To the student brought up on romantic theories of poets and poetry, the biography of John Milton, like that of the other two greatest poets of the English language—Chaucer and Shakespeare, must be disappointing. For all three men lived lives too ordinary to seem suitable for poets. Chaucer earned his living most of his life as a civil servant, for a while as a customs clerk. Shakespeare retired from his profitable career as a playwright to live out his life peacefully in Stratford and willed his wife his second-best bed. And Milton, in some ways, departs even farther from the picture we cherish of the poet: the man tormented by conflicting passions who cannot live in a world too insensitive to understand him. Not only did Milton never become a beatnik; he never even had any reason to. If he was not a rebel in our sense of the term, however, he was, nonetheless, a man of stern integrity and firm independence.

MILTON'S BIOGRAPHY

MILTON'S BACKGROUND: John Milton was born in 1608 into a Puritan family. His father after whom he was named, was a scrivener, a recorder of property deeds and titles. The family was highly cultured, for Mr. Milton was a fine musician, a composer who attained some recognition among his contemporaries. He was evidently aware of his son's exceptional gifts and provided him not only with an excellent education but also with sympathetic understanding.

Milton attended St. Paul's School in London, one of the best secondary schools of the day. He received additional instruction from a tutor at home, a young dissenting clergyman named Thomas Young, who became one of Milton's good friends. Milton concentrated on Latin and Greek and was taught Hebrew as well. He managed also to learn Italian very well, though no modern languages were taught either at St. Paul's or at Cambridge, which he entered in 1625.

He enrolled in Christ's Church College at that University and became one of its distinguished students, even though he was "rusticated" or suspended for a time because of a sharp disagreement with his tutor, William Chappell. He took his bachelor's degree in 1629, the same year in which he wrote his first really famous English poem, a Christmas ode entitled "On the Morning of Christ's Nativity." It is probable, also, that during his later years at Cambridge he wrote *L'Allegro* and *Il Penseroso*. These companion poems—"The Cheerful Man" and "The Pensive Man"— are probably the first works of Milton that the American student reads. They contrast two ways of life or, perhaps, two moods. The first celebrates the light-heartedness which seeks innocent pleasure. The second describes the more serious pursuits of the thoughtful man.

MILTON'S VOCATION: In 1632, Milton completed his M.A. and went to live at Horton, his family's country retreat. He remained there for six years, pursuing a diligent course of reading and writing in order to prepare himself to be a great poet. For Milton had decided when he was very young that poetry was the vocation to which he was called. And to the devout son of religious parents, one was called to his vocation, whatever it might be, by God.

In 1638, Milton left Horton to make the "grand tour," the step which was to complete his elaborate preparation for his career. He traveled principally in France and in Italy. The tour was cut short by rumors of civil war in England. Milton returned to England in 1639, the date of the First Bishop's War and the beginning of the Puritan Revolution.

During all these years Milton had been supported by his understanding and indulgent father. But upon his return from the Continent, both father and son seemed to think that it would be a good idea if the younger John began to earn his own living. He established himself in London as a schoolmaster, with his nephews, John and Edward Phillips, as his first two pupils.

Milton soon became involved in the religious debates of the day. His inclination was toward the Puritan party. The Puritans found the Church of England too broad and too Catholic in using a rich liturgy and vestments. They wished to purify the church from within on the basis of scriptural principles and to do away with bishops and the support of the church by the state. As a Puritan, Milton was opposed to church government by bishops and wrote several pamphlets advocating the abolition of the episcopacy.

MILTON'S MARRIAGES: During the 1630's there was a power struggle between King Charles and his Parliament. After the Long Parliament of 1640, the king was deprived of some of his power, and Parliament undertook church reform along Puritan lines. In 1642 the Parliamentary party demanded control of the army, the privy councilors, and even the education of the king's children. It is curious that Milton, a strong Puritan, in this year married Mary Powell, a member of a Royalist family whose support of the king was in opposition to Milton's support of the Puritan and Parliamentary cause. Mary, who was younger than he was and used to a large, cheerful household, left him after a very short time to visit her family, a visit that was to continue for three years, partly because Mary wanted to stay with her family and partly because the Civil War, which began August 22, 1642, made it quite difficult for her to return to London.

She did return, though, in 1645, and the two were reconciled. She bore her husband three daughters and a son who died in infancy. She died herself in 1652 in giving birth to the third of the daughters. Milton married again in 1656, this time to Katherine Woodcock, whom he loved very much. She died, also in childbirth, less than fifteen months later, and her child lived only a month. One of Milton's most beautiful sonnets, "On His Deceased Wife," commemorates their brief marriage. Milton's third and last marriage, in 1663, to Elizabeth Minshull, was very frankly a marriage of convenience. The poet, who had been blind by then for 11 years, needed someone to run his household and help rear his three occasionally rebellious daughters.

MILTON'S POLITICAL ACTIVITIES: Milton continued during the early years of the Civil War to write pamphlets on the controversial issues of the day. His first volume of poems was published in 1645. The volume is of major importance because it includes both *Comus* and *Lycidas,* two of Milton's great works. However, the next period of Milton's life was devoted not to the poetry he loved but to a duty he felt to be more immediately pressing: the duty of doing what he could to establish and maintain the Puritan Commonwealth.

The first phase of the Civil War had ended in 1645 with the defeat of Charles I at the Battle of Naseby. But hostilities were renewed in 1648, and in 1649, Charles I was beheaded. In that same year Milton was engaged as Latin Secretary to the Council of State of the Commonwealth, a Council which Oliver Cromwell headed. Since Latin was the language of diplomacy in the seventeenth century, his office required Milton to write whatever letters were sent to other governments. He was, besides, expected to defend the regime against its numerous enemies in print. As a consequence, he became involved in pamphlet wars which he found sometimes demeaning and always time-consuming. The greatest of his prose works was written against Cromwell's government, rather than in its behalf, and was ignored in Milton's day. That work is *Areopagitica,* Milton's impassioned defense of freedom of the press. The reader of *Paradise Lost* might be interested also in *De Doctrina Christiana (On the Christian Doctrine),* a treatise on theology which throws some light on the intellectual background of Milton's greatest poem.

MILTON'S BLINDNESS AND DISILLUSIONMENT: It was during his service to the Commonwealth that Milton became blind. The disability came upon him gradually, but Milton did not allow it to interfere with the heavy reading and writing that his position demanded. By 1652, however, he was totally blind, and it became necessary for others to share in his labors. His blindness occasioned one of the most moving of his sonnets, "When I Consider," written in 1655. It records his fear that he will never be able to use his God-given gift for poetry again. Yet God may demand an accounting from him, for his entry into Heaven will depend upon how well he has used the gifts God gave him. The sonnet ends with Milton's acceptance of the fact that what God wants of him is obedience and resignation. He can, then, serve God even if he can't write poetry, for "they also serve who only stand and wait."

In 1658 Cromwell died and was succeeded by his son, Richard, who was quite incapable of ruling in his father's stead. Thus, in 1660, Charles II, of the House of Stuart, the son of Charles I, whom Cromwell had beheaded, was restored to the English throne. Milton's life was in very real danger, and he was for a short time imprisoned. After his release he lived in disillusionment and bitterness. The Commonwealth, he had long realized, was not the Utopia for which he had worked. But in restoring the Stuarts to the throne, in no longer trying to live in a republican state, his people, he felt, had turned their backs on freedom. Milton was alienated from the most powerful elements of the society of the time also because the Stuarts and their followers stood for the institutions he had fought against most of his life: the monarchy and the episcopacy. He expresses his sense of being an exile in the beginning of Book VII of *Paradise Lost,* in the invocation to Urania.

This last period of his life was, nonetheless, his most creative. For it was during these years, in which he felt himself to be the prophet who had failed, the man of the Lord to whom no one listened, that he completed his greatest works: *Paradise Lost, Paradise Regained*, and *Samson Agonistes*.

MILTON'S MINOR POEMS

ON THE MORNING OF CHRIST'S NATIVITY (1630):   Milton
wrote his friend Charles Diodati that this poem came to him on
the morning of Christmas Day and that it was his "birthday gift
to Christ." It was his first finished and serious work. Four stanzas
in rhyme royal introduce the hymn itself. This is the birthday of
Christ "of wedded maid and virgin mother born," who will atone
for man and "with His Father work us a perpetual peace." For
us he laid aside heavenly majesty and became mortal. The poet
hopes to present his poem before the Wise Men come, for he knows
he cannot compete with their treasures. Then begins the hymn
itself. The babe lies in the rude manger, while Nature has put
off her gaudier dress in sympathy with him. She is clad only in a
white robe of snow. Universal peace descends and no sound of
war is heard. The night is peaceful when "the Prince of light/His
reign of peace upon the earth begins." The stars in amazement
gaze steadfastly. The sun hides his head for shame at seeing a
greater Sun appear. The shepherds sit "simply chatting in a
rustic row," unaware that mighty Pan (Milton uses this classical
name for Christ) has come to live on earth. Heavenly music
sounds, and cherubim and seraphim sing heavenly music, only
made before when the sons of the morning sang while God set
the constellations and hung the world in its place. If such music
rings out again, time will run back and "fetch the Age of Gold,"
when Truth and Justice with Mercy between them may come to
earth. But Fate says this is not to be yet—the Babe is still an
infant who "on the bitter cross/Must redeem our loss." At "the
world's last session," God will come as Judge and The Dragon
(Satan) will swing his tail in fury to see his kingdom fail. The
pagan deities do not dare stay, now that the Babe shows his true
Godhead. Now the Sun in bed "pillows his chin upon an Orient
wave" and night's chariots cross the sky. The "Virgin blest" has
laid her Babe to rest. The youngest star is poised in the heavens
and bright angels in order sit around the stable.

L'ALLEGRO AND IL PENSEROSO: The date of this delightful pair of poems is uncertain. E. M. W. Tillyard has plausibly suggested that they were written in Cambridge c. 1631 for an academic audience. In this case, the opening lines of *L'Allegro* in particular, previously puzzling because so bombastic and so different in style from the rest of the poem, are explained as deliberate parody of the classical poems which the Cambridge students were obliged to imitate. "Directly they heard of Melancholy being born of Cerberus and blackest Midnight—infamous coupling—they would have a comfortable sense of recognition and begin to grin."

The two poems contrast a gay mood with a serious one. In *L'Allegro*, the dismissal of Melancholy is followed by an invocation to Euphrosyne or Mirth, who brings with her merry companions "Quips and Cranks and wanton Wiles,/ Nods and Becks and wreathed Smiles," Sport and Laughter, who is holding his sides with glee. As they trip it "on the light fantastic toe," L'Allegro joins them and hears the sounds of morning. The lark sings, the cock crows, the horns of the hunters blow, the plowman whistles, the milkmaid sings, the mower whets his scythe. Around him is the lovely pastoral scene, with the sheep nibbling on the lawn, the clouded mountains, the daisied meadows, and a castle half-hidden in the distant trees. Shepherds eat their mid-day meal by their cottage, bells ring, and rebecks (a form of violin) sound, as youths and maidens dance until the daylight fails. In the evening over "spicy nut-brown ale" the peasants tell tales of Queen Mab and her doings and of Puck, the "lubber fiend." The peasants go to sleep, but L'Allegro does not, for "Tower'd cities" please him, and "the busy hum of men." He may go to the theatre to see plays by Jonson or Shakespeare (or perhaps he reads these works). Calling on "soft Lydian airs" which will soothe him against care and worry, L'Allegro enjoys music which brings back the story of Orpheus and Eurydice. This song ends his day, and L'Allegro concludes

> These delights, if thou canst give,
> Mirth, with thee, I mean to live.

In *Il Penseroso*, the poet turns to more somber moods. Though this poem is a little longer, the scenes develop in the same succession as in *L'Allegro*. Dismissing "vain deluding Joys," the speaker hails "divinest Melancholy," born of Vesta and Saturn (this is Milton's invention). The "pensive Nun, devout and pure,/ sober, steadfast, and demure," clad all in black, is so still that she looks like a marble statue. Like Euphrosyne, Melancholy has her companions, Peace, Quiet, Fast, Leisure, Contemplation, and

Silence. As in *L'Allegro,* there is birdsong, but this time Philomela (the nightingale) sings her even-song. While the poet wanders on the smooth lawn to watch the wandering moon "stooping through a fleecy cloud," he hears "the far-off curfew sound . . ./ Swinging low with sullen roar." Inside, "where glowing embers . . . Teach light to counterfeit a gloom," where the cricket chirps and the bellman cries the hours, Il Penseroso enjoys his midnight studies. He studies Hermes Trismegistus (the supposed author of books of mingled magic, philosophy, and astrology), and calls down the spirit of Plato to be his companion. As in *L'Allegro,* drama is mentioned (and here it is likely that the speaker reads rather than sees the plays), but now it is "gorgeous Tragedy" which enthralls him, tales of Thebes, or of Pelops' line, or of ancient Troy. He reads also Chaucer's half-told tale "of Cambuscan bold,/ of Camball and of Algarsife," i.e., *The Squire's Tale* in *The Canterbury Tales,* one of the more serious chivalric romances. Like L'Allegro, Il Penseroso thinks of the music, especially that of Orpheus, such notes as "drew iron tears down Pluto's cheek." At length "civil-suited" (i.e., sober) morning appears, but the speaker does not wish to be exposed to the full rays of the "day's garish eye" but to walk in "arched walks of twilight groves," where he may hear the hum of the bees and the murmur of the waters, dream to their music, and wake to hear harmonies not usually heard by mortals. Then he will "walk the studious cloister's pale," admire the arched roof and the "storied windows richly dight,/ Casting a dim religious light," and hear the pealing organ and the singing of the choir. This music will bring heaven itself before his eyes. He hopes that he may ponder the meaning of the stars and the herbs "Till old experience do attain/ To something like prophetic strain." (This section, lines 155-174, has no parallel in *L'Allegro.*) The poem closes with a couplet:

> These pleasures, Melancholy give,
> And I with thee will choose to live.

THE SONNETS (Various dates):   Milton wrote twenty-four sonnets of which five are in Italian. Some were conventional addresses to friends or acquaintances, some (such as the one on his blindness and the one to his dead wife) are very personal. Others are addressed to political figures of the day, such as General Fairfax, Cromwell, or Sir Harry Vane, or allude to recent events, such as the slaughter of the Vaudois by the Duke of Savoy in 1653. The sonnets have been carefully studied by John Smart, in his *Sonnets of Milton* (Glasgow: Maclehose, Jackson and Co., 1921), which may be referred to for details.

Perhaps the most effective of the personal sonnets is #15, usually called "On His Blindness." This allusion to his blindness is the first of many in his poetry. "The present poem," says Smart, "composed when the calamity was fresh, and before he had become accustomed to a life in darkness, opens with a mood of discouragement and grief, and closes with quiet resignation." The sonnet is based on the parable of the talents (Matthew 25: 14-30) in which the unprofitable servant was punished for burying, not using, the talent his master had given him. Milton wonders, now that blindness has fallen upon him before half his working life is spent, whether God will still expect him to use his talent: "Doth God exact day-labour, light denied?" Patience replies that while God does not really need "Either man's work or his own gift," He wants obedience and resignation. Thousands of angels serve Him, but men "also serve who only stand and wait." Milton is thinking that there are angels of contemplation as well as of action; similarly, some men may serve God best who humbly accept His decrees, waiting in faith on His will. Smart quotes many scriptural passages which Milton may have had in mind, such as "Rest in the Lord and wait patiently for him" (Psalm 37:7).

Connected with Milton's service to the State as Latin Secretary is the magnificent sonnet "On the Late Massacre in Piedmont." On April 24, 1655, the Piedmontese, at the order of the Duke of Savoy, had slaughtered about 1712 harmless people living in the Swiss Alps. These were the Vaudois or Waldensians, a medieval sect which rejected the use of good works for the dead and laid great stress on restoring Gospel simplicity. They had lived for centuries in their isolated community, pursuing their own religion, until suddenly and barbarously attacked by the Piedmontese. Protestants all over Europe, who regarded the Vaudois as true primitive Christians, were shocked. Cromwell took up their cause and official protests were sent, not only to the Duke of Savoy, but also to Protestant governments in Denmark, Sweden, The Netherlands, and the Swiss Protestant cantons. It was Milton's task as Latin Secretary to compose these letters. He also expressed his own personal sense of shock in this sonnet. He calls on God to avenge the slaughtered Vaudois, who had been preserving Christianity in a pure state when our English ancestors had been worshipping "stocks and stones" (i.e., images in the medieval church). The suffering of this true flock of God ("thy sheep") should be recorded in God's book, as "in their ancient fold" they were killed by the savage Piedmontese, who even hurled a mother with an infant in her arms from the rocks. (This is a reference to an actual incident; see Smart, p. 106.) The valleys re-echoed the groans of the sufferers to the hills, who in their turn sent them to heaven. Milton begs that, as the blood of martyrs is truly held to be the seed of the church, the blood and ashes of these martyrs may be sown in Italy, where the Pope ("the triple tyrant"—a reference to the Pope's triple crown) still reigns. From this seed may come a new crop of converts, who, having learned God's true ways "early may fly the Babylonian woe" (i.e., to Milton—the false Catholic church).

MILTON'S MAJOR WORKS

COMUS (1634):   When Milton wrote this work at the request of Henry Lawes, a noted musician of the day, he entitled it "A Mask." In 1738, long after Milton's death, it was given the name by which it is now known by one of its printers, Dr. John Dalton.

A mask was a sort of Renaissance musical comedy. Masks were written to be presented in the homes of wealthy patrons of the arts. They were usually pastoral in nature. That is, they imitated the pastoral poetry of the Greeks. They had rural settings and often had as their characters shepherds or shepherdesses with Greek names. According to the tradition of the pastoral, these shepherds could sing and write poetry as well as herd sheep. The masks included songs, dances, and spectacle, but had intellectual content as well. In Milton's mask the intellectual content is far more important than the other elements, though the poetry is lyric and the piece has several graceful songs, for which Henry Lawes wrote the music. *Comus* was written to be presented at Ludlow Castle by the children of the Egerton family, assisted by Henry Lawes. The father of the family, the Earl of Bridgewater, had at that time recently been appointed the President of Wales.

Comus opens with a speech by the Attendant Spirit whose business it is to guard the two sons and the virgin daughter of the family. The three children are approaching the castle through some woods. They may be in danger because of Comus. He is the son of Bacchus, the Greek god of the harvest, and Circe, the sorceress who turned the followers of Odysseus into pigs. He is himself a magician, and when he gets people in his power, he gives them the heads of beasts. They are unaware of the change they undergo because their bestiality consists of overindulgence in animal pleasures. The Attendant Spirit takes the form of Thyrsis, one of the family's shepherds.

Thyrsis is right about the danger. The two brothers have left their sister, the Lady, as she is called in the mask, while they go to find her something cool and refreshing to drink, for she is very tired. They are gone so long that she starts to look for them. She calls out for them in a lovely song, which Comus overhears. He sends his band of rioters away. Assuming the disguise of a simple shepherd, he approaches the girl. When she tells him why she is alone, he tells her that he has seen her brothers in a nearby cottage. In her trusting innocence, she goes with him.

Meanwhile her brothers have begun to look for her. The younger brother is afraid that she has fallen into some danger. The elder brother says that there is no need to worry because she will be protected from serious moral danger by her chastity. The younger brother feels, nonetheless, that she may suffer from an outside force, even though her virtue protects her soul. As it turns out, both brothers are right.

The Attendant Spirit, Thyrsis, finds the two young men and leads them to where Comus has imprisoned their sister. She is seated on a chair from which she cannot move, and Comus is trying to make her swallow the drink that will place her under his power. She refuses and argues so convincingly that too much self-indulgence is wrong that Comus temporarily sways toward her opinion. He recovers himself, though, and offers her the drink again. Before she can reply, her brothers rush in and break the glass containing the potion. Comus and his band flee, but the Lady is still chained by enchantment to the chair, for the brothers failed to get Comus' magic wand with which they could release her.

Thyrsis calls upon Sabrina, a nymph who is the guardian of the local river and a staunch supporter of chastity, to free the Lady. Sabrina answers his call, and the mask ends in rejoicing when Thyrsis leads the three children to their parents' castle.

Comus contains some of the elements which are to be found in *Paradise Lost*. The Lady, like Eve, follows her tempter because, in her innocence, she sees no reason to suspect him. Unlike Eve, however, the Lady does not succumb to temptation. Her virtue, her chastity, protect her inner freedom so that her soul remains her own. Thus, the Elder Brother, who said that her innocence was her shield against moral danger, was right. But her innocence has also led her into bodily harm. She is not physically free after her encounter with Comus. An outside force, Sabrina, who respects the chastity that the Lady has sought to preserve, has to free her. Thus, the Second Brother, as he is termed in the mask, is right, too. Milton, then, in this early discussion of freedom seems to be quite sure that man's ultimate moral responsibility rests in his own power. He is realistically aware, though, that outward circumstances play their role in human life, too.

One other way in which the temptation in *Comus* differs from the one in *Paradise Lost* is in the character of the tempter. Comus is far more amiable and attractive than Satan is. He wishes the Lady to do wrong, but he seems to be much more an Epicurean, a believer in the delights of the senses, than he is a devil or a principle of wickedness.

LYCIDAS (1637): *Lycidas* was written as part of a memorial volume Cambridge University published in honor of Edward King. King, a student slightly younger than Milton, was drowned when the ship on which he was sailing to Ireland struck a rock and capsized. King was at that time only 25 years old. He had been ordained a minister and was something of a poet as well.

Milton used this combination of circumstances to good purpose in *Lycidas*. The poem is highly traditional. It follows the conventions of pastoral poetry, in which one shepherd sings a dirge for a fellow shepherd with whom he has shared his pastoral duties. But "shepherd" or "pastor" among Christians is a traditional name for a priest. Since Edward King was both priest and poet, Milton is able to synthesize his mourning for King with a consideration of what a priest ought to be and of what a poet's function is. He comes to the conclusion that though the poet will not really find his place in nature or under paganism, he has a true home in the Christian world touched by the grace of God.

PARADISE REGAINED: *Paradise Regained* was completed in 1666 or 1667, but was not published until 1671. It is a short epic, and in it Milton was probably imitating *The Book of Job,* which had been considered an epic since the time of St. Jerome in the fourth century. The subject matter of the two books has much in common. Job is tempted to deny God and conducts debates with his short-sighted friends who try to persuade him to be untrue to himself. In *Paradise Regained* Christ, tempted by Satan, debates with the Devil. Like Job, he stands firm in his obedience to God.

Milton's primary source for *Paradise Regained* is the account of Christ's three temptations by the devil in the Gospel according to Saint Luke.

BOOK I: Christ goes into the desert to meditate upon his vocation after He has been baptized by St. John the Baptist on the banks of the River Jordan. St. John declares Christ to be the Messiah, and his statement is confirmed by God. For the Holy Ghost, at Christ's baptism, descends in the shape of a dove and a voice from Heaven declares that Christ "is My beloved Son, in whom I am well pleased."

Satan had beheld the baptism. He confers with the other devils, as he did in *Paradise Lost,* and determines to find out if Christ is really the Seed of the Woman, Who is to bruise his head. He wants also to tempt Christ away from His mission, as he tempted Adam and Eve. God watches the devil's meeting from Heaven and assures the angels that Satan's temptation will bring Christ glory.

Satan approaches Christ in the shape of an old man after Christ has fasted for forty days and nights. Satan suggests that Christ turn the stones into bread so that they and other residents of that wilderness can eat. Christ reminds him that man does not live by bread alone but by every word that proceeds from the mouth of God. He mentions, too, that He recognizes Satan. Satan admits his identity, but says that even though he cannot be saved, he often carries out the commands of God. Also, he sees that Christ is good and beautiful and says that he would like to be with Him. Christ, unlike Eve, is not moved by Satan's flattery. He tells Satan that the devil can go or stay, as he chooses, because nothing Satan does is done without God's permission.

BOOK II: Satan travels again to the "middle region of thick air" where the devils are meeting. They are no longer confined to Hell because Adam and Eve succumbed to temptation. Satan tells his fellows that Christ is not going to be so simple to defeat as Eve was. Therefore, Satan will need whatever help they can give him if he is to succeed. Belial suggests that Satan try tempting Christ with beautiful women, since in Belial's experience that method always works. Satan assures Belial that in Christ's case it won't work. Christ is much too noble to succumb to temptations of the flesh and too determined to fulfill his mission.

Christ, meanwhile, has slept and has dreamt of food, but He awakens to the knowledge that His long fast continues. Satan comes to Him again and offers Him miraculously a beautiful banquet. Christ refuses, saying that He will accept nothing from Satan. Christ could Himself order such a banquet in the wilderness, but its excessive luxury is loathsome to His temperate nature.

Satan sees that he cannot destroy Christ through food. He offers, then, to help Him get all the riches of the world. Christ will need riches, he says, if He is really to fulfill His destiny as king of the Jews. He can have wealth if He follows Satan, whereas "virtue, valor, wisdom, sit in want." Christ says that wealth without these virtues is meaningless and that it is better to give up a kingdom than to seize one in the way the Devil urges.

BOOK III: Satan next urges Christ to seek an empire for the sake of glory, but Christ assures him that glory among men is meaningless. The only glory He wants is to be approved of by His Father in Heaven. Even though Christ wants no glory, He is, as Satan says, destined by God to restore the throne of David and to reign for all eternity. Since that is His destiny, He shouldn't wait but should accept Satan's help in order to achieve His end as soon as possible. Christ replies that He will achieve His destiny in the fullness of time. He wonders why Satan so wants to hurry Him since Satan's dominion will end as soon as His begins. Satan replies that since he has no hope, he has no fear. If he must be ruled, he feels he'll do as well as possible under the mild reign of Christ.

Then he says that Christ hasn't seen enough of the world to be prepared for His destiny. He takes Him, therefore, to the top of a high mountain from which He can see all the kingdoms of the earth. Satan offers Him first the Parthian empire and its military might. Christ says that He has no desire to conquer by force. Nor does He need military might to free the Jews who have been dispersed because they practiced idolatry. They will return and be part of His kingdom when they return to the worship of the true God.

BOOK IV: Satan, very much worried by Christ's firmness, next shows Him the wealth and luxury of Rome and says that, with Satan's help, Christ can easily gain that empire. Christ rejects Rome, too. Satan, with the impudence of despair, says that he is not offering Christ these kingdoms for nothing. They are His, if he will fall down and adore Satan. Christ refuses, saying, "Thou shalt worship the Lord thy God, and only Him shalt thou serve."

Satan next offers Christ the wisdom of Athens, which He will surely need if He is to rule His kingdom well. Christ assures Satan that the wisdom of the ancient world is known to Him. If He forsakes the truth of the Bible to pursue that wisdom, it will prove to be not wisdom at all but only a delusion.

Satan returns Christ to the wilderness, saying that such a barbarous place is best suited to a man who has refused all that civilized human beings pursue: wealth, honor, arms, the arts, wisdom, and glory. He warns Christ, however, that the Savior will be sorry for refusing Satan's gifts. Christ falls asleep in the wilderness unsheltered from the violent storm that Satan, in his anger, sends upon Him. Morning comes, and Christ awakens to a world that seems the fresher because of the storm. Satan comes again and finds Christ unperturbed by the night's disturbances. The Fiend shouts at Him in rage: "I doubt that you are the Son of God. All the angels and all men are sons of God. I was termed Son of God once myself. How do you differ from the rest of us? I'll make you prove whether or not you really are the Messiah."

He carries Christ to the pinnacle of the tower on top of the Temple of Jerusalem. "Now," he says, "stand there if You can. If not, cast Yourself down. For if You really are God's Son, He'll send angels to protect You lest You 'dash Your foot against a stone.' "

Christ says to him, "Tempt not the Lord your God." Satan, in amazement, falls to the earth. The angels come to minister to Christ and to proclaim His glory. When He has been refreshed, He returns quietly to His mother's house.

> **COMMENT:** Paradise, according to Milton, is regained when Christ practices perfect obedience, just as it was lost when Adam disobeyed. In this poem, as in *Paradise Lost* and *Comus,* Milton is interested in man's freedom in the face of temptation. The guile of the serpent is frustrated because Christ is truly wiser than Satan and truly stronger.
>
> Christ's last words to Satan, "Tempt not the Lord thy God," have a double meaning. Christ is saying that He will not tempt God by accepting Satan's dare. He will not prove His divinity to the Devil by throwing Himself from the tower on the presumptuous hope that God will rescue Him. He is similarly taunted at the Crucifixion when the rabble yell, "If You are the Son of God, come down from the Cross." Christ refuses then, too, for His divinity is to be established by His obedience to His Father, not by means of grandiose gestures.
>
> The other meaning of the words is the meaning which silences Satan. Christ is declaring His own divinity to His tempter. He is reminding Satan that his ultimate act of presumption, his attempt to make God do Satan's will, will recoil upon his own

head. Satan will suffer more for this last, most insolent attempt to make himself greater than God than he has for any of his other wicked deeds. Satan set out to discover whether or not Christ is the Messiah sent to destroy him. He wanted to defeat Christ, too, if he could. To his sorrow he has discovered that Christ is, indeed, the same Son Who defeated him in the battle in Heaven. (See Book VI of *Paradise Lost*.)

SAMSON AGONISTES: There is some doubt about the exact date of composition of Milton's last work, *Samson Agonistes*. It was first published in 1671 with *Paradise Regained*.

Its form is the form of Greek tragedy, though the poem is not meant to be presented on the stage. Its action takes place in one day, and it has only one setting, as is true of most Greek tragedies. The violent action, also according to Greek tradition, is reported rather than presented. The play also has a chorus, as did the Greek tragedies. The Chorus comments on the action and fills in background the reader needs to know.

The source of the tragedy is the Old Testament account of Samson. It can be found in the *Book of Judges*, chapters XIII-XVI. Samson was a Nazarite, one chosen by God to help to free the Israelites from their enemies, the Philistines. One of the vows the Nazarites took was never to cut their hair, and the secret of Samson's strength lies in his long hair. In the Biblical account, during Samson's early career, he is strong and playful in his use of his strength. Milton makes Samson's early achievements more noteworthy than they are in the Bible. In both the Bible and in Milton, the Philistines set out to discover the source of Samson's strength through his Philistine wife, Dalila. She tries four times to find out. The first three times Samson lies to her and has ample opportunity to learn that Dalila wants the information in order to betray him. Nonetheless, he tells her the truth the fourth time. The Philistines, while he is asleep, cut his hair and blind him. He is enslaved and put to work in a Philistine mill in Gaza. The play takes place on a festival day in honor of Dagon, the Philistine god; hence Samson does not have to work.

Samson Agonistes, the title of the play, means Samson the wrestler or athlete, for "agonistes" comes from "Agon," the Greek word for contest. In the seventeenth century the word had nothing to do with "agony" or inner torment.

SAMSON'S DESPAIR: The action of Milton's play takes place within Samson himself. It begins with Samson in despair. He has failed entirely to achieve his people's freedom. All he has succeeded in doing is destroying himself. He mourns his blindness in passages which are justly famous. He can admit that he deserves the punishment he suffers, but he can see no point to his life. Why was he chosen to be his people's champion if he was to end as a slave to their enemies?

He is visited by a chorus of men from his tribe, the tribe of Dan, who offer him kindly sympathy. Then his father, Manoa, comes. He tells Samson that the festival the Philistines are celebrating is to honor Dagon for having delivered Samson, the champion of the Hebrew God, into their hands. Both father and son mourn the fact that Samson's foolishness has led the Philistines to mock not only him and his people but also God. Samson sees in this event, though, his first ray of hope. The issue now is drawn not between Samson, God's champion, and Dagon, but between God, Himself, and Dagon. And God will not be mocked.

Manoa goes to try to arrange ransom for his son, though Samson would prefer to suffer the punishment he knows he has earned. His next visitor is Dalila. She comes gorgeously dressed, followed by a train of women. She asks Samson to forgive her, offering him a spate of contradictory excuses for her conduct: she was intimidated by her countrymen; she was urged to betray Samson for patriotic reasons; she betrayed him because she loved him—if he were weak and blind, he would have to stay with her instead of endangering his life by fighting. She ends by asking Samson to come to live with her and allow her to care for him. He turns aside all her arguments and rejects her offer with contempt. Balked in her plans, Dalila shouts in rage that she will be recognized as a heroine by her people for all time because she has destroyed the mighty Samson.

Samson's next visitor is Harapha of Gath, a giant. He regrets that Samson is blind, he says, because he would have liked to defeat this great champion of the Israelites in combat. Samson offers to fight Harapha anyway, saying that he will meet the fully armed giant with only a staff as a weapon. Harapha accuses Samson of gaining his victories by means of magic spells. Samson replies that his only helper is God. He tells Harapha to go pray to Dagon and then return to fight him, the champion of God. Then Harapha will discover where real power rests, whose god is really God. Harapha taunts Samson again with his plight, but though Samson repeatedly challenges him, the giant refuses to fight. Afraid of even a blind Samson, Harapha withdraws, shouting threats.

Next a public official comes with a message from the Philistine lords commanding Samson to perform feats of strength at the festival in honor of Dagon to amuse the guests. Samson at first refuses indignantly to use his gifts for so contemptible a purpose. Then, feeling within himself an inspiration that suggests he may be able to use the opportunity to win glory for God, he offers to go. He departs, telling the Chorus that they will hear of him:

> Nothing dishonourable, impure, unworthy
> Our God, our Law, my nation, or myself. . . . (11. 1424-1425)

SAMSON'S DESTINY FULFILLED: When Samson has departed, Manoa returns, eager to tell the Chorus the progress he has made in seeking his son's release. As he and the Chorus speak, they hear first a shout of glee when the Philistines catch sight of their enemy in chains. Then the Israelites hear a terrible roar. A Hebrew messenger comes to tell them that Samson has killed all of the residents of Gaza by pulling down the temple of Dagon in which they were gathered. He tells Manoa that Samson could not perform his feat except at the cost of his own life.

The Chorus and Manoa are struck with wonder at Samson's deed. The Chorus praises Samson and laments his death, but Manoa sees that the occasion is not one of sorrow. Samson has fulfilled his destiny. He has freed his countrymen and brought honor to them and to God.

> **COMMENT:** Samson moves from the despair he feels at the beginning of the poem to complete confidence in his ability to achieve the destiny for which he was born. The change takes place in the course of the three interviews that constitute the body of the play.
>
> In his interview with his father, Samson realizes that though he has made a fool of himself, he cannot make a fool of God. If the issue is clearly drawn between God and Dagon, God has to win. In other words, Samson's earlier conviction that he has failed God, that his actions have brought shame upon God, is a conviction that is rooted in pride. God doesn't *need* Samson. He can choose other means to achieve His ends. Hence, nothing Samson has done has really damaged God. Samson's insight,

then, is both a source of humility and a source of faith. The despair of the early part of the poem is groundless, for Samson needn't rely only on Samson. He can rely on God.

His encounter with Dalila is, it would seem, a means whereby he regains some faith in himself. He has been fooled by this woman—almost willingly fooled, but he will not be fooled again. He has gained mastery of himself.

He no longer desires her so much that she can persuade him to do what she chooses. He has the very real satisfaction of seeing *her* lose control. She exits screaming insults because her softer weapons no longer work.

By the time Harapha arrives, Samson's poise has been restored. The taunts of the cowardly giant are hollow, and Samson has no trouble seeing Harapha's weakness or parrying Harapha's insults. If Harapha is Dagon's champion, then surely Dagon is not well served. Nor is Harapha much of an enemy for Samson. The real enemy, the real giant, was Samson's despair. Samson can manage Harapha, the huge blusterer, because he has already wrestled with his own despair. In his blindness he "sees" more truly than he saw when he had eyes. His ability to recognize spiritual reality is his largest gain. He "sees" through Dalila, and he "sees" through Harapha because he has "seen" through his own despair. He has discovered how much of that despair was based on pride, and he has remembered the strength of his God.

Thus, when he is commanded to use his strength to entertain the followers of Dagon, he is prepared for his destiny. He knows that God can use even the blinded Samson. And he trusts himself enough to recognize the inspiration God has sent him. He knows that the inner voice to which he listens is not the voice of his own pride. It is the voice of God. Hence, he can say with confidence that the Chorus will hear nothing about him that is in any way shameful. He no longer sees himself as God's champion. He is rather God's instrument. And when he places himself in the hands of God, he can do nothing but succeed. Now that he recognizes humbly that none of his exploits were ever really his own, that all of his strength was really God's strength, he has gained the kind of moral strength he needed if his physical strength was to accomplish anything of value. Now that he knows himself to be God's instrument, he cannot fail to be God's champion, too.

Samson Agonistes, like *Comus* and *Paradise Regained*, shares themes found in *Paradise Lost*. In *Paradise Lost*, Adam and Eve succumb to temptation, as Samson did. But through repentance and the grace of God, they rise, as Samson does, to heights they never could have reached before.

PARADISE LOST

INTRODUCTION: *Paradise Lost* was originally published in ten books in 1667. In its second edition, that of 1674, two of the original ten books were divided to form the twelve-book poem we know today.

Milton had intended to write an epic most of his life, for to men of the Renaissance the greatest poetic form was that of the epic. Milton had originally planned to use King Arthur as the subject of a poem that would glorify England as Virgil's *Aeneid* glorified Rome. He changed his mind, however, and chose a topic of wider significance: a topic that included in its span the whole human race, since we are all children of Adam, and which glorified not a nation but God himself.

We do not know the exact date at which Milton began his greatest work, but we do know from Milton's comments within the poem that it was written after he had become blind. Milton composed his poem in his mind in segments, having trained himself to remember them. Then he dictated these passages to a secretary.

The poem is written in blank verse—unrhymed lines of iambic pentameter (lines of five feet, each foot containing two syllables, the second of which is accented). It is a verse form which permits the narrative sweep Milton needed for his subject. The reader need not pause at the end of each line as he would have to do if the lines rhymed. Furthermore, Milton had no need to break his poem into the small units a stanzaic pattern would have required. Thus, some of the paragraphs of *Paradise Lost* are long and complex. Others are short and direct. Only blank verse could have given the poet so flexible a medium.

PARADISE LOST AS AN EPIC: An epic poem is a narrative poem of considerable length which tells a story of great importance. Its theme should be significant to all men, and its readers should be profoundly aware of the grandeur of its subject. In other words, an

epic cannot treat of trivial matter. And its style must permit the
reader to feel awe, to be caught up in the perception of events of
great magnitude, of suffering that makes his own seem less worth
worrying about. No reader of *Paradise Lost* can fail to see that
Milton's poem fulfills these requirements.

Besides modeling his poem in its general outlines upon the *genre*—
the type of poem—he thought to be of greatest stature, Milton
made use of epic conventions that men of the Renaissance considered traditional. The reader's ability to grasp these conventions
will depend upon how many epics he has read and how well he has
read them. For instance, the beginning of the poem is an epic con-
vention. Homer's *Iliad*, the first great epic, begins with a request
to the Muse to sing of the wrath of Achilles. Furthermore, Milton,
in the beginning of his poem, states his subject—"man's first disobedience" and the consequent loss of Paradise. Homer's subject
was the wrath of Achilles and its consequences. The *Aeneid* begins:

> Arms and the man I sing who earliest came
> Fate-bound for refuge from the coasts of Troy
> To Italy, . . .   (tr. by T. H. Delabére-May.)

The subject of the poem, of course, is Aeneas' voyage to Italy and
his conquest of that land after the fall of Troy.

There are other echoes of earlier epics in Milton's poem, too. The
single combats between Satan and Michael the Archangel and between Satan and Abdiel in Book VI echo both the *Iliad* and the
Aeneid. So do the games of skill that the devils in Hell play in
Book II. However, for most readers Milton's imitation of these
epic conventions is of much less importance than is his use of his
source material from the Bible. The reader should be familiar at
least with the first three chapters of *Genesis*. He will find the King
James version most helpful because that is the version Milton used,
and he often quotes from it directly.

ALLUSIONS TO OTHER WORKS: Milton is a learned poet, and
his learning has been an obstacle to many modern readers. Milton
used his learning, however, not to make his work confusing but to
make it richer and more meaningful. Furthermore, most of the
allusions Milton makes to other works would have been familiar
to readers of his own day. Twentieth-century readers, however, need
to read *Paradise Lost*—and Milton's other works—in a well an-
notated edition. An edition with exceptionally helpful notes is
Paradise Lost and Other Poems, edited by Edward Le Comte (New

York, 1961). *Milton: Poems and Selected Prose,* edited by Marjorie Hope Nicolson (New York, 1962), and *Paradise Lost,* edited by Merritt Y. Hughes (New York, 1962), are useful, too.

Milton's learning shows not only in his references to other works but also in his style. He knew Latin well enough to have written many poems in that language and to have considered using it as the medium for his major work. His decision to use English instead has enriched our language indeed, but these riches are such that they require some effort on the part of the reader if he is to enjoy them fully.

UNRAVELING THE STYLE: Milton's style is commonly said to be Latinate. That is, instead of using the common English sentence pattern of subject-verb-object, Milton uses more elaborate patterns drawn from Latin. He is very fond of inversion, for instance, of beginning a sentence with a prepositional phrase, with the object of the verb, or with the verb itself. Of course, the sentences of other English writers do not always begin with the subject either, but few other authors use the sort of sentence structure habitual with Milton.

Milton's style may, therefore, seem difficult at first. The student can teach himself to read it, however, fairly readily. He needs simply to parse some of Milton's sentences, to find their subjects and their verbs, until he acquires an ear for Miltonic English just as he once had to acquire an ear for spoken English. For instance, look at the sentence in Book I beginning in the middle of line 45:

> Him the Almighty Power
> Hurled headlong flaming from th' eternal sky
> With hideous ruin and combustion down
> To bottomless perdition, there to dwell
> In adamantine chains and penal fire
> Who durst defy th' Omnipotent to arms.

The verb of the sentence is "hurled," and its subject is "the Almighty Power." "Him," the first word of the sentence, is the object of "hurled." "Who durst defy th' Omnipotent to arms" modifies "him" (who is Satan, as we know from the context of the sentence). The most difficult element of the sentence to place correctly is "with hideous ruin and combustion." It is an adverbial phrase modifying "hurled." In other words in normal English order the sentence would read as follows:

The Almighty Power, with hideous ruin and combustion,
hurled him, who durst defy the Omnipotent to arms,
headlong flaming from the eternal sky down to
bottomless perdition, there to dwell in adamantine
chains and penal fire.

The process will seem hard at first, but in a short while most students
find Milton's verbs and nouns as readily as they find them in their
daily newspapers.

One cannot deny that Milton's style presents problems. However,
the student who reads Milton's poetry carefully will find that once
he has become accustomed to its mannerisms, it is really not hard
at all. Milton's is, furthermore, a style most students find tremen-
dously exciting and eminently satisfying. Reading the poem aloud
will, of course, help to develop an ear for Milton. It will, in addi-
tion, open up for the reader the richness of tone he misses if he
reads with his eye alone. *Paradise Lost* is poetry that should be
heard as well as seen.

DETAILED SUMMARY

PARADISE LOST—BOOK I

(Lines 1-26) Milton begins his poem by announcing its theme: the
story of how Adam and Eve ate the fruit of the tree of the knowledge of good and evil. In doing so, they brought sorrow and death
into the world and lost for men their place in Paradise, a place
which was regained only through Christ, the "greater Man" of
line 4. Milton, like the ancient writers of epics in whose footsteps
he is following, asks the Heavenly Muse for help. He uses the name
the Greeks had given to the nine goddesses of inspiration, the
mythical figures who explained in pagan terms the mystery of
human creativity. Milton, however, shows that his prayer is really
directed to the Judaic-Christian God because the Muse turns out
to be the one who inspired Moses, the traditional author of the
first five books of the Bible and the first person to teach the Jews,
the chosen people of God, to explain to them how God made the
world. Milton needs the inspiration of God Himself, because he
has chosen to sing of the highest possible subject, the providence
of God. If he really is to make clear the "ways of God to men," he
will need God's help to understand his theme and to express it
effectively.

(Lines 27-124) The story begins with Satan, whose name means the "Adversary." For it is Satan who deceived Eve. Satan was once Lucifer, the highest angel in Heaven. In an attempt to make himself equal to God, he had rebelled and had persuaded one-third of the angels of Heaven to rebel with him. But he and his whole force were defeated by God and the angels who had remained true to Him. The rebels, thrust into Hell, have lain in torment on a burning lake for nine days. Satan, moved still by pride and by a desire for revenge, raises his head and looks about the hideous prison for which he has lost Heaven. He sees his second-in-command, Beelzebub, and addresses to him a speech of proud rebellion. He and Beelzebub, he says, are united in misery as they were once united in the "glorious enterprise" to dethrone God. God may have proved Himself the stronger, but Satan will not repent, nor will he cease to defy God. Though the field is lost, he will plan revenge. He will never bow down to God. Why should he when God so recently went in terror of him, doubting that He could hold His empire against Satan's power? In spite of the great loss they have suffered, Satan's forces are still strong and still immortal. And their experience has made them wiser. They will know more now about how to war against the tyranny of God.

(Lines 125-191) Beelzebub, in despair, asks how either their strength or their immortality are to profit them or hurt God since they must suffer eternal punishment in Hell. Satan assures him that no matter what happens, the fallen angels in Hell will never do the will of God. They will devote their whole intelligence to evil. They will do their best to destroy the good things God makes. When God tries to bring good out of evil, they will pervert His ends and bring evil out of good. Satan notices then that God has apparently recalled His troops. Since, therefore, they are at least temporarily free, he suggests that they move from the burning lake to a nearby plain where they can more comfortably consider how to carry on their war against God.

(Lines 192-241) During this exchange with Beelzebub, Satan has been lying with only his head lifted, the rest of his body stretched out on the lake. He is as large as the monsters who in pagan myths were said to have warred against Jove (the highest god in the Roman religion). He is as huge as Leviathan, the whale. Yet if God had not permitted him to rise from the burning lake, he would have been compelled to remain there forever. God has allowed him to rise only because his continued defiance gives God the opportunity to be merciful to Man, whom Satan will seek to seduce. Satan can permanently injure only Satan with his malice. Satan

and Beelzebub rise and fly to dry land—which is burning, just as
the lake was—and rejoice because they think they have escaped
the fiery flood by means of their own power.

(Lines 242-330) Satan looks about Hell again, mourning its ugliness, but vowing that it is better "to reign in Hell than serve in
Heaven." For, according to Satan, God rules in Heaven as a tyrant.
Since Satan and his followers are really God's equals in nature,
God reigns not through right but only through the force of arms.
Beelzebub has by now cheered up a bit, and the two of them move
with great pain across the burning floor of Hell to rouse the rest
of their army. The other fallen angels lie sprawled upon the lake
of fire in complete confusion. Satan calls to them in a speech that
resounds through Hell. Are they enjoying their rest on such a bed?
Or does their "abject posture" mean that they are worshipping
their Conqueror? God's troops, finding His enemies thus defenseless, will trample upon them or with thunderbolts fix them forever
to the bottom of the pit. "Awake, arise, or be forever fallen!"

(Lines 331-521) Shamed by Satan's cry, the other angels spring
to attention like well-disciplined soldiers and begin to collect themselves into military formation. Milton uses this opportunity to comment on their number and to name the more important fallen
angels, who are now devils. The names he uses are not those they
were given in Heaven, for those names have been forever blotted
out. The devils are called, rather, by the names of the pagan gods
who figure in the Old Testament: Moloch, Astarte, Thammuz,
Belial, etc. The devils, Milton is saying, carried on their war against
God by leading people away from Him and setting themselves up
as gods in His place. Milton, thus, recalls the continuing battle
between good and evil, between God and those who have rebelled
against Him. The details of this battle would have been very
familiar to the readers who lived when Milton did, for everyone
knew the Bible extremely well. The list, therefore, gives Milton the
chance to suggest the inevitable outcome of Satan's decision always
to fight God. For the accounts of the pagan gods must necessarily
include or recall the deeds of the prophets or heroes who were the
instruments God used to defeat His enemies and the enemies of
His chosen people, the Israelites. Thus, Milton mentions the good
king Josiah when he tells about Moloch, and none of his first readers
would have failed to think of Samson, who destroyed the temple of
Dagon, when Milton comments on that god of the Philistines. (For
the story see the *Book of Judges.*) Christ, who will ultimately
accomplish Satan's total defeat, is referred to twice when Milton
mentions "that opprobrious hill" and "that hill of scandal." He

means the Mount of Olives on which Christ was betrayed by Judas. Such an act would seem to proclaim Satan's power over the world. It is, however, the act in which God most resoundingly brings good out of evil. It is the beginning of the sacrifice by means of which Christ redeemed mankind.

(Lines 522-621) Satan's followers gather before him. They are obviously disheartened but show signs of being cheered by Satan's courage. He's a bit doubtful himself, but recalling his pride, he comforts them with high-sounding but empty words. Trumpets sound, and Azazel, his standardbearer, unfurls Satan's banner. The troops of lesser devils, with a ringing shout, in turn raise their banners, their spears and shields. They march in perfect order, their pain soothed by music, and come to a halt directly in front of Satan. He reviews his troops with an experienced military eye. As he sees their numbers and their strength, he grows even more proud and more determined to defy. God than he has already been. For never has any man at any time seen so powerful and so magnificent a host. Satan, even though his glory has been dimmed, shines above them all. His eye, though cruel, is clouded with remorse when he looks upon those whom he has led to destruction. He is so much moved by their pain that at first he cannot speak because of his tears.

(Lines 622-669) Mastering himself, Satan speaks to his followers much as he has already spoken to Beelzebub. They have lost a glorious battle, he says. But how could they have foreseen that a host so glorious and so powerful as the one they formed could have been defeated? Furthermore, since they were strong enough to empty Heaven, surely they will be strong enough to regain their place in Heaven. After justifying his leadership and his courage, he tells his followers his plans. Now that they know God's strength, they will not provoke Him to open warfare. They will try to achieve their ends by fraud. Perhaps their first "eruption" will be to investigate the new creation that was rumored in Heaven: new worlds peopled with a new race. Hell cannot hold the devils long. There will never be peace because they will never submit. Thus, their only choice is to declare eternal war. The other devils, shouting their defiance of God, approve his words by flourishing their flaming swords and clashing their shields.

(Lines 670-798) Then led by Mammon, the fallen angel who had had an eye for gold rather than for God even in Heaven, the devils discover on a nearby hill some of the mineral resources of Hell. With incredible speed and artistry, a palace rises on that same hill.

It is called Pandemonium, a word Milton made up that means "all the devils," just as "Pantheon," the name of a temple built in pagan Rome, means "all the gods." Meanwhile heralds call the devils to a conference to decide how best to carry out their war against God. Most of the devils reduce themselves in size so that all of them can fit inside Pandemonium. In an inner chamber, the principal devils, as large as ever, begin their meeting.

COMMENT: Satan in Book I of *Paradise Lost* is in some ways an appealing figure. Most of us admire the rebel, especially the rebel who will not bow down to another even in defeat. He is a good military leader. And when he feels sorrow at the sad plight of those he has led to so terrible a punishment, we cannot but sympathize with his state of mind. But Milton does not intend us to see Satan as a hero. He is at the most noble in Book I because he is still close to his original state, and he had been the most beautiful angel God created: Lucifer, son of the Light. But even in Book I the effects of his sin are beginning to show. He blusters. He presents the commonest excuse the wrongdoer who has failed can make: he says more than once that he had no way of knowing God was so strong when he rebelled since no one had ever tried His strength. He lies when he claims to have emptied Heaven, for only a third of the angels rebelled. The rest of the poem, especially Books V and VI, will reveal other lies, too. And he is a fool. In spite of the terrible defeat he has just suffered, he refuses to acknowledge the power of God. He will continue the battle, even though he should realize that all he can get out of his fight is further pain for himself and for his fellows. But he insists upon deluding himself. Milton is careful to tell the reader that Satan and his host can rise from the lake of fire only because God permits them to. Yet, though Satan has every reason to know that truth, he and Beelzebub rejoice in their strength as if they had struggled up through their own power. It should not come as a surprise, therefore, when some of Satan's most moving words turn out to be true in a way he does not intend. Remember, particularly, lines 254-255:

> The mind is its own place, and in itself
> Can make a Heaven of Hell, a Hell of Heaven.

Satan means that his strength and the strength of his followers can achieve serenity even in Hell. The reader, in Book IV, will discover that the words really mean something quite different.

Since Milton announces his theme in Book I, he obviously wants his reader to think about what it means throughout the book. He has said that he intends to "justify the ways of God to men." The word "justify" can mean simply that Milton intends to prove that God is just, that his decision to force Adam and Eve out of Paradise was not unfair. But Satan has said that he is going to turn all God's good to evil, to destroy the good things God has made. Hence, Satan will win if Adam and Eve are merely punished, no matter how well deserved the punishment may be. God must do more than be fair. To defeat Satan He must bring good out of evil. He must turn all of Satan's attempts to do evil into something really good. Otherwise the "justification" will not be complete, and Satan will truly have won. "Justify" in the poem, therefore, must have a positive as well as a negative meaning, a positive meaning the reader should be alert to discover.

PARADISE LOST—BOOK II

(Lines 1-42) Satan sits on his richly beautiful throne. His determination to go on fighting against God has raised him to this "bad eminence." His despair has, in a sense, placed him higher than hope could have done, for hope would have led him to a second place in Heaven. Despair has raised him, ironically, to the first place in Hell, the peak of evil, which is, of course, at the same time, the lowest possible spot in the universe. He begins the conference of the principal devils by assuring them once more that they will regain Heaven and be more glorious in their rise than if they had never fallen. They have an advantage over Heaven, for the unfallen angels can envy God and the Son and covet Their glory. But Satan's position is secure. He is the leader of the devils through nature, through the "fixed laws of Heaven." But his fellows have also chosen him as their leader because of his merits. Besides, his position is not one to be envied. He stands between the other devils and the wrath of God and is condemned to endure the deepest pain. Since the others surely feel they are in sufficient pain already, there can be no faction in Hell based on envy, because there is nothing to envy but pain. "We are sure to prosper," he says, "but how are we to do it—by open war or by sabotage?"

(Lines 43-105) The first to speak is Moloch. A strong, obstinate bully, he can see no possibility of achievement except through the use of brute force in open war. He admits he's not much good at clever tricks. But why waste time on them? Why sit in the awful hole that is Hell, waiting for stratagems to be devised? The devils can use the fire and brimstone, the instruments God has invented to torture them, as weapons against God. They can drown Him and His forces in sulphurous flames. It will be easy to ascend again to Heaven, for their natural motion as spirits is up, not down. They have no need to fear defeat, for they can't possibly be worse off than they are right now. If God annihilates them, they need fear no more pain. If it's true that they can't be annihilated, then they will retain at least the power they have now. And they know they have enough power to disturb God, if not to conquer Heaven. Thus, they will have at least revenge, even if they can't achieve victory.

(Lines 106-228) Moloch resumes his seat, frowning and threatening—especially those who are not so strong as he. The next speaker is Belial, a clever, lazy coward. His manner is graceful and pleasing. He would be for open war, he says, if the best warrior among them had not urged war simply out of despair. The devils will, according to Moloch, achieve either annihilation or revenge. But what revenge is possible for them? Heaven is well guarded. Even if they do succeed in reaching and attacking its ramparts, God cannot be injured or destroyed. He would soon cast off Hell's fires and emerge once more victorious. And in His anger, He would destroy the devils completely. Belial would rather exist in pain, than not exist at all. Besides it's possible that God can't destroy the devils. And even if He could, would He be likely to let them off so easily? Would He dissolve them utterly instead of reserving them for endless punishment? "Things aren't so bad now," says Belial. "Here we are fully armed, discussing our plight. Remember when we fled from God's forces and thought that Hell was a refuge from His thunder? Remember how dreadful it was on that lake of fire? If we even think about war, God may grow still angrier at us and make us suffer pangs seven times worse than the worst we've already endured. We can't fool Him. He'll discover any plots we make. Let's accept the chains we have instead of inviting worse. It takes just as much courage to endure our punishment as it took to rebel. Besides, if we sit here quietly, God may forget about us and stop fanning those terrible flames. Or we'll get used to the climate and come to find it mild. And we can hope for better things in the future if we don't make matters worse by annoying God even more." Thus Belial urges not peace, which would mean real repentance, but a cowardly withdrawal.

(Lines 229-298) Mammon, the next speaker, says bluntly that the devils can't hope to disenthrone God. Therefore, they can't hope to regain Heaven. If God should offer them pardon, none of them would much enjoy singing His praise or acknowledging His power, "So let's forget about Heaven and make the best of Hell. We don't need to worry about the darkness of Hell. Heaven, after all, is sometimes dark with clouds, too. Besides, if we investigate carefully the mineral resources of our region, we'll find plenty of gems and gold to give us light and other material, too, to build a kingdom that will rival God's. Our torments will seem like ease once we get used to them. So by all means, let us forget about war. Let's see what we can do to lessen our pain and establish a nation here in Hell." The other devils like Mammon's advice. They want no more of God's thunder or of the sword of St. Michael, the Archangel who leads God's host. And the prospect of rivalling God by means of their own empire in Hell, an èmpire built slowly and *safely*, is indeed inviting.

(Lines 299-389) Then Beelzebub, Satan's second-in-command, rises majestically to speak, commanding the attention of the whole counsel. "Are we now to be called Princes of Hell," he asks, "instead of by our heavenly titles? You are deluding yourselves if you think we can quietly build a comfortable empire in this place. God has ordained it to be our prison. His curb upon us may seem right now to be far away, but don't fool yourselves. He intends to remain sole King of the Universe, including Hell. We are silly to debate about whether we want war or peace. We have been sent here because we made war and lost. We have been offered no terms of peace, nor have we sought them. For we know that peace between us and God is meaningless. The only terms we will be offered are slavery, eternal punishment. The only peace we can return is a desire for revenge. We seek only the means to make His conquest as bitter as possible to our Conqueror. We will not need to launch another direct attack against Heaven. There exists an easier enterprise. God swore by oath to create a new world peopled by a new race—man—whom He will love more than He loves us, even though this new creature is to be less than us in glory. Let's discover, then, how we can best subdue the new world. It is God's outpost and, as such, will surely be easier to assault than His citadel itself. We can lay this world waste with hell-fire, or take possession of it, or drive its feeble inhabitants into Hell as we were driven. Perhaps we can seduce them to our side, make their Creator their foe, as He is ours, so that He will destroy them Himself. To hear His puny 'darlings' curse their Creator should spoil His joy in our overthrow. Could there be a sweeter revenge for us? Wouldn't such a plan be better than brooding here in the darkness hoping to hatch 'vain empires'?"

Beelzebub's counsel, first suggested by Satan, wins the devils' full assent.

(Lines 390-429) Beelzebub praises their "godly" decision, which perhaps, he adds, will take them near enough to Heaven to re-conquer it. Or, if not, they will at least be able to dwell in a milder zone wherein their grievous wounds can be healed. He asks, then, for a volunteer to spy out the new land, not only to brave God's watching angels but also to dare to cross the unknown terrain which lies between Hell and the "happy isle." Such a messenger will carry their last hope of success. The devils eye one another in silent dis-may until Satan, in the splendor of native majesty that raises him above his fellows, speaks.

(Lines 430-505) "I do not blame your silence in the face of this challenge. Hell is enclosed by nine fiery walls, and gates of burning stone forbid the messenger to leave. Should he be able to pass them, he will find himself on the edge of the abyss of Old Night—a bottomless chaos, empty, trackless. If he can conquer chaos, he enters an unknown world from which it may be just as hard to escape. But I would be a poor king indeed, were I to refuse to undertake anything necessary to the public good, no matter how frightening it may be. Therefore, I'll go. The rest of you stay here and do whatever can be done to make Hell a pleasanter place to live. I'll undertake this mission alone." Rising, Satan closes the meeting abruptly so that none of the other devils can win easy fame by offering to go when he knows his offer will be refused. The others fear Satan, however, as much as they fear the journey. They rise, too, bow toward their leader as if he were God, and praise his courage in one voice. Only men, says Milton, perpetually dis-agree, since even the devils in Hell occasionally enjoy concord.

CELEBRATION IN HELL:
(Lines 506-628) The results of the Council are trumpeted through-out Hell by four cherubim and are acclaimed by the whole of Satan's host. The devils, temporarily cheered up by false hopes, try to while away the time until Satan's return. Some hold races or practice war games. Others tear up rocks and hills from the floor of Hell and raise a wild whirlwind in a desire to forget their troubles. Quieter spirits sing ballads of their battles, glorifying their deeds and com-plaining about the unjust fate which has defeated them. Philosophic devils engage in futile, but enticing debate, on "providence, fore-knowledge, will, and fate." Four squadrons of devils set out to ex-plore Hell to see if any part of it offers a pleasanter place to live

than the region in which they found themselves at the end of the battle. Each squadron explores in vain the banks of one of the rivers that flow into the burning lake: Styx, the river of hate; Acheron, the river of sorrow; Cocytus, the river of lamentation, and Phlegethon, the river of rage. Far away from these hellish rivers is Lethe, the river of oblivion. Beyond its banks lies a frozen continent. Milton says that one of the punishments of the souls to be sent to Hell will be to suffer first the heat of the fiery rivers and then the cold of the icy land. As the damned cross Lethe between the two extremes, they will try desperately to drink of its water, but they will not be able to. Their punishment will lie in the torments of their conscience, torments which will not permit them to forget their sins.

(Lines 629-680) Meanwhile, Satan flies alone to the gates of Hell. The boundary walls of Hell are built clear up to its roof, and its gates, circled with fire, have nine layers—three of brass, three of iron, and three of adamantine rock, rock too hard ever to be broken. A guard sits on either side. On one side is Sin: a beautiful woman from the waist up, but an ugly serpent below the waist. A circle of hellhounds races howling about her middle. If anything disturbs them, they kennel in her womb, still barking and snapping in rage. On the other side of the gate is Death, shapeless, dark, huge, and hideous, with the "likeness of a kingly crown" upon what "seemed his head." He strides toward Satan, shaking Hell as he moves. Satan is astonished at the sight, but, fearing only God and His Son, he addresses the monster bravely:

(Lines 681-726) "Who do you think you are to try to bar my way? I'll pass through those gates no matter what you do. Give way, or find out what happens when the likes of you attacks one who is heaven-born!" Death mockingly retorts that Satan, the leader of the rebels, no longer has the right to call himself a Son of Heaven. Threatening new pains for the devil if he refuses to obey, Death tries to shoo him back into the depths of Hell. As Death speaks, he swells tenfold and becomes ten times more ugly, too. Satan, still unafraid, faces him, and the two prepare to annihilate one another, when Sin intervenes.

(Lines 727-814) "Satan, you strive to kill your only son. Son, you seek to destroy your father. And whom are you serving by your deeds? Him Who sits in Heaven and laughs at you as you do His bidding, knowing that in the end He will destroy you both anyway." Death withdraws at her words. Satan, surprised, says he will withhold his blow till he finds out what she means by calling him her father and saying that Death is their son. He disclaims any connection with her, saying, "I've never seen anything so hideous as the two of you."

WHAT SATAN HAS STIRRED UP: "Have you forgotten me, Satan?" she asks. "I didn't seem ugly to you when we met in Heaven at the assembly of angels conspiring to rebel. Remember the terrible headache you had, the flames which shot forth from your brow until the left side of your head opened, and I sprang, fully armed, into being. The other angels fell back in fear, but after they'd got used to me, they found me quite attractive. You, especially, liked me because I was your perfect image. We took our joy in secret, and I became pregnant. Meanwhile you fought and lost the war. When the rest of you were thrown into Hell, I was, too. Given the keys to Hell, I was charged never to open its gates. It was there that I gave birth to that monster you see. When I saw him brandishing his fatal dart, I cried out, 'Death,' and the name echoed through Hell. He pursued me, raped me, and from our incestuous union came these hounds you see who torture me, egged on by Death. He would like to devour me, since his appetite is insatiable. But he knows that if I die, he will die, too. Do not fight him, Father, for no one can resist him except the One Who reigns above."

(Lines 815-889) Satan speaks more gently now to his daughter-wife. His errand, he says, is to free both her and Death as well as the other devils. He is going to find the "upstart race" rumored in Heaven. It has been created to replace the fallen angels and provide God with more docile subjects in case more of the angels rebel. When he returns, Sin and Death may live at ease in the new world he is setting out to conquer. The two listen to his words with hideous glee. Sin says, "I'll not obey the Ruler Who hates me and Who forbade me to open these gates. I'll listen to you, my author, who will soon bring me into the light and at whose right hand I'll reign without end." She opens the gates, but she has not the strength to close them, and they remain open wide enough for an army to march easily through.

(Lines 890-987) Satan and his family look out upon a sea without bound and without order, a sea where Night and Chaos reign in eternal anarchy, where the elements of the material world we know—"Hot, cold, moist and dry"—war with one another instead of being formed into an orderly cosmos. Satan pauses before venturing into the abyss, with its tumultuous noises, but finally he leaps into it and traverses its wild confusion afoot, on the wing, sometimes flying, sometimes crawling. At last he comes within earshot

of the worst hubbub of all. Making his way toward this spot to ask
directions for the nearest shore, he finds himself at the throne of
Chaos and of his consort, Night. Their courtiers are all those things
which lead to chaos in human society: Rumor, Chance, Tumult,
Confusion, Discord. Satan asks these powers to help him find the
new world whose territory God has wrested from Chaos. It is his
intention, he says, to destroy that world, to return it to the kingdom
of Night. He isn't interested in territory, only in revenge.

(Lines 988-1055) Chaos, "the Anarch old," has heard of Satan and
has rejoiced in his rebellion, for it brought "confusion worse con-
founded," just the state of affairs that suits Chaos best. Telling
Satan the journey is nearly over, he carefully gives the devil the
advice he seeks, because to Chaos "havoc, and spoil, and ruin" are
pure gain.

Satan moves on eagerly, though with intense effort, through the
void. But after the fall of man, Sin and Death will come from Hell
and build a highway over Chaos, across which devils will pass with
ease to tempt and to destroy the souls of men. Satan glimpses dim
light and travels with less pain, and finally with ease, until he can
see again his former home and at last his goal: the World we know
suspended near the moon from a golden chain. He hurries toward
it, possessed with his desire for revenge.

> **COMMENT:** Even if we knew nothing of Milton's political
> career, we would realize that he must have had some experience
> with bureaucracy at work because of the realistic committee
> meeting which is the first episode of Book II. The principal
> devils are readily recognizable types of human beings. Moloch
> is the bully, the man who understands only force and who
> cannot speak without shouting threats. Milton's republican
> spirit delighted in stressing the etymology of the name, for it
> means "sceptred king," and Moloch's character reflects quite
> accurately what Milton thought of kings in general. Moloch's
> bully-like character coincides, too, with his activities as pagan
> god in the Old Testament. His was a cult that required its
> adherents to slay their firstborn children in his honor.
>
> Belial, who speaks next, is the sly coward. He is suave. He
> flatters Moloch, calling him the best warrior of their host. His
> advice to the devils to try to appease God by keeping quiet is
> presented, as such advice often is, with face-saving eloquence.
> We can almost see him finger his discreet mustache and smile
> winningly at his fellows as he deprecatingly offers his modest

suggestion. He is not a false god in the Old Testament. He figures there, rather, as the personification of pagan ungodliness.

Mammon, in turn, is the blunt business man, the pragmatist with an eye for the main chance. As we were told in Book I, even in Heaven he was more interested in the gold pavement than in God and his fellow angels. What, then, does he care about Heaven and its glories when he sees all the untapped mineral resources of Hell? The absolute character of his materialism is what makes him an ultimate enemy of God. To love wealth as he loves it shuts out all possibility of spiritual or moral life. Thus, Christ in the New Testament tells His disciples they cannot serve both God and Mammon. (Mammon, again, is not a pagan god, but the epitome of avarice.)

But it is in Satan's manipulation of the meeting that Milton shows himself to be indeed aware of the limitations of democratic processes. Book I makes it clear that Satan, when the meeting began, already knew what he intended to do to gain his revenge against God, but instead of presenting his plan directly, he plants his stooge, Beelzebub, in the audience. The other devils have their say, and when it looks as though the Belial-Mammon faction has won, Satan's lieutenant speaks powerfully and persuasively. The devils agree and give Satan a mandate to do what he had planned to do anyway. The group has not come to a real decision. It has been wangled into agreeing with the decision Satan had already made. Satan's next step is amusing and, like many other things in the poem, it contradicts his words. At the beginning of the meeting he had told the devils that there could be no envy in Hell, But when he has volunteered to go as a spy to earth, he ends the meeting abruptly, fearing that the other devils might enviously try to steal his glory.

The Allegory of Sin and Death: The allegory of Sin and Death at the end of Book II is not only impressive and powerful, but also very important to the themes of the poem. The figure of Sin is psychologically true. We are frightened when someone first suggests that we do wrong, just as the rebel angels were frightened at the first sight of Sin during their assembly in Heaven. As we think, though, about the fun we could have if we simply didn't obey the rules, the wrong which at first was frightening becomes attractive, just as Sin was attractive to Satan in Heaven and as the upper half of her body is still attractive when she guards the portals of Hell. But when we yield to temptation and actually do wrong, we discover the ugliness of sin, as she is ugly from the waist down. And we discover the bitter consequences of sin, that its fruits can lead to death of the spirit, to the kind of remorse that gnaws at one's conscience without offering the possibility of repentance or relief, just as the hellhounds gnaw at the womb of Sin and yet cling to her.

Theologically, the allegory is quite apt. It is Sin only that can open the gates of Hell. The only way to enter that citadel is to sin. It is Sin and Death who build the easy highway between earth and Hell, for yielding to temptation has never been really difficult for men. Similarly, it is Sin who gives birth to Death, because in the Judaic-Christian tradition, it is because of sin that we are subject to death. This aspect of the allegory is true in another way, too. The kind of evil-doing that Milton means by sin is soul-killing. To become involved in sin, to be committed wholly to evil, is to kill off all that is human, all that is good in our souls. The career of Satan in the poem illustrates that meaning of sin and death. Satan, created by God, is ordained by nature to know the truth and to be good. He demonstrates his natural affinity for the good and the true by his horror when he first sees Sin and Death at the gates of Hell. They *are* ugly, and he is so much aware of their ugliness that he must be persuaded before he can acknowledge them as his responsibility and accept them as his own offspring. Notice his contrasting reaction when in Book IV he sees Adam and Eve for the first time.

Death is, perhaps, even more horrifying than Sin. She may be monstrous, but she is at least shaped. Death is formless, without outline or essence, devouring whatever it comes upon, turning its victims into nothingness. Because it simply destroys what it eats rather than converting its food into its own substance—an action Death cannot perform because it has no substance—it is forever hungry, made hungrier, for that matter, by the very victims it wolfs down. The figure, as Milton presents it, is the stuff of our worst nightmares, the nameless, shapeless, horrible less-than-something that seeks to shove us, too, into the nothingness we fear.

The Unholy Trinity: It is the thematic significance of Satan, Sin, and Death, however, that is most important. Sin comes into existence fully grown as she leaps from the head of Satan. That is theologically true, for sin was born when Satan, the first sinner, rebelled. But no reader in Milton's day would have missed the fact that she is born of Satan as Athena in Greek mythology was born of Zeus. Zeus, to Christians of the Middle Ages and the Renaissance, was an analogue of God the Father. The Greeks, in their search for truth, had discovered, in these men's eyes, enough about the nature of the universe to have a foreshadowing of revelation. They were aware that there is a supreme being, even if they were not entirely right about the nature of this being. Satan, then, since he has a relationship to Zeus, must also have a relationship to God.

What Milton is developing becomes clearer when we consider more thoroughly Sin's relationship to Satan. Satan did not create her. She sprang full-grown from his head. Now, there is a Person whom God did not create: the Second Person of the Holy Trinity, the Son Who becomes Christ, and Who is, in theology, said to be God's only begotten Son. Sin and Satan are of the same substance, then, just as God the Father and God the Son are. Milton would seem, therefore, to be establishing a second trinity, an unholy trinity in opposition to the Holy Trinity.

But a trinity means that there must be three persons. The Third Person of God's Trinity is the Holy Ghost. He is, in Christian doctrine, the love which binds the Father and the Son. And it is by means of the Holy Ghost, or Love, that the world was created and that men on earth both know and love. He is the Spirit Who moves across the waters and makes them bear life in the opening verses of *Genesis*.

There is a third person in Satan's trinity, too. Death is born of the incestuous liaison of Sin and Satan, a relationship characterized not by love, but by lust at first, by hate later. Death, however, is just as much the bond between Sin and Satan as the Holy Ghost is the bond between God the Father and His Son.

Milton's Parody: Milton, then, has quite deliberately established a parody of the Holy Trinity. The Satanic trinity destroys, just as the Holy Trinity creates. Its members are held loathsomely together by hate, as the Members of the Holy Trinity are bound by Love. And its activities are as ugly, as slimy, as self-destructive as Milton can make them. Death rapes Sin—thereby committing incest, just like his father—and begets the hellhounds who gnaw at her vitals. Death refrains

from destroying Sin only because he knows that when she dies,
he will die, too. There will be no more death when there is no
more sin.

The final point which establishes the unholy trinity most unmistakably comes at the end of the speech in which Sin agrees to
open the gates of Hell for Satan. She says, in lines 868-870, that
Satan will bring her into bliss, "where I shall reign/ At thy right
hand voluptuous, as beseems/ Thy daughter and thy darling,
without end." In the Nicene Creed, a summary of Christian
doctrine, known to every Christian of Milton's day, it is said
of Christ—the Son—that "he sitteth at the *right hand of the
Father*. And He shall come again with glory to judge both the
living and the dead; of whose kingdom there shall be *no end*.'

Milton's invention is daring, so daring that it may even seem
to be blasphemous. Why does he devote such care to it, making
it as clear and as powerful as it is? It is his dramatic way of
stating as emphatically as possible the theme of his poem. He
is telling of the battle between good and evil, between God
and an anti-god. The anti-god will do anything in his power
to destroy God's creation. He wants to return what God has
made to the dominion of Chaos, the confused un-being which
existed before God's creative act informed it and made it the
beautiful cosmos we know. To choose between good and evil,
Milton is saying, is to choose between God's creative trinity
of love and Satan's destructive trinity of hate.

Chaos: Chaos helps Satan, even though the reader is aware
that Satan has lied to him: Satan has told his fellow devils that
he seeks dominion over the new world, but he tells Chaos he
wants only revenge. Their ends do coincide, however, because
wherever Satan introduces Sin and Death, the territory of Chaos
is extended, no matter whether Satan keeps the nominal power
in his own hands or not. Milton, in picturing Chaos, encountered
a real technical difficulty. How does a poet create chaos and
still maintain the order without which there would be no poem?
It isn't enough to say that Chaos and his domain are noisy and
chaotic. The reader must be made to experience that noise and
chaos. Milton accomplishes his end partly in his account of
Satan's painful journey over the confused void with its meaningless obstacles and sudden pits, its ceaseless cacophony. The
speech of Chaos is a subtler means. Chaos speaks rather
bumblingly: "I know thee, stranger, who thou art" (ll. 990).
The simple, unrepetitious way of saying that is, "I know who

you are, stranger." The "thee" and "who," both of which redundantly mean the same thing, provide a chaotic grammar for the chaotic speaker. The rest of his speech is marked by meaningless inversions and awkward statements of simple ideas, too.

Just as in Book I, Satan in Book II says something the reader should remember because it later turns out to be true in a way Satan doesn't intend. Note well that he tells the devils at the beginning of their conference that

> from this descent
> Celestial Virtues rising will appear
> More glorious and more dread than from no fall,
> And trust themselves to fear no second fate: (ll. 14-18).

PARADISE LOST—BOOK III

(Lines 1-55) Book III begins with Milton's address to "holy light," holy because it is, in *Genesis,* the first thing God created. It is, in fact, so holy that St. John says "God is light." Milton has traveled, he says, through the darkness of Hell and of Chaos into the light of Heaven, where he feels God's light even though his physical blindness is so complete that no light visits him. Though he is blind, he still practices his poetic art, as Thamyris and Homer, ancient poets, did. He mentions, also, two blind prophets of antiquity, Tiresias and Phineus, since, for Milton, one of the functions of poetry is to prophesy. The poet must bear witness to the truth just as the Old Testament prophets did. Milton laments his blindness with touching pathos, saying that one avenue to truth is quite shut off for him. He asks, therefore, that the "Celestial Light" inspire him the more to know and express truth *not* visible physically. In the next section of the poem, Milton explains God's reaction to the events in Books I and II.

(Lines 56-134) God, seated on His empyreal throne with His Son at His right hand, looks down upon His works. He sees Adam and Eve happy in Paradise and then looks toward Hell. He sees Satan just as that devil has passed Chaos and is coming upon the edge of this world. He speaks to His Son, telling Him that Satan has escaped his prison and is on his way to seduce Adam and Eve. God knows, furthermore, that man will fall. But he will fall, says God, through his own fault. God has given him sufficient strength and grace to withstand Satan and to keep the one law that has been imposed upon him. But since God has also given man free will, he can fall if he chooses to. If man and the angels had not been created free, there would have been no merit in their praise of God and their obedience to Him. They would have served not Him, God says, but necessity. And even though He foreknows the fall of both men and angels, they cannot say they were predestined to fall, for His knowledge does not *cause* their fall. The only way in which God could have prevented the fall of the angels and of men would have been to change their nature, to make those He had created to be free into slaves. Since Satan and the other devils tempted and depraved themselves, they deserve no mercy. But since man will fall because Satan will deceive him, God will extend mercy and grace to him.

(Lines 135-166) All of the angels rejoice at God's words of mercy. In the Son, God's glory shines with utmost radiance when He praises the Father for extending grace to man, whose folly should not be punished as severely as the devil's fraud is punished. If it were to be, Satan would defeat God's ends. No matter what further punishment God inflicted upon him, Satan would have triumphed. Either the whole human race would be drawn into Hell with Satan, or if God were, in His anger, to annihilate men, He would be destroying His own creation.

GOD'S PROMISE RENEWED:
(Lines 167-216) God again promises grace to man. He will save those who want to be saved. He will enable them to stand against the devil. And their ability to be true will come so unmistakably from God that no man will be unaware of how weak his fallen nature would be without God's help. God will save all those who accept His grace and show that they want salvation by performing acts of prayer, repentance and obedience. He will give them Conscience as a guide. He will turn away only those who willfully turn from Him. But since Adam *will* sin and will try to be like God, some expiation must be made. Otherwise the claims of divine justice will not be satisfied. Man will be so' imperfect because of his sin that he, alone, will be unable to atone for his fault. Therefore, men must die unless someone will die for them, someone whose nature is such that he will be able to make full recompense for man's offense. Who, then, will take this burden upon himself?

(Lines 217-265) The heavenly host is silent. Man would have been doomed to eternal death had not the Son made Himself man's Intercessor and Redeemer. "Man will find grace," says the Son, "because I shall take on man's nature, permitting death to wreak his full vengeance on me. I shall not dwell long in death's power. I share Your Life, Father. After death has had all of me that he can lay claim to, I shall rise again, despoiling death of his victim. Thus, I shall kill death, and shall lead Hell captive in spite of all that Hell can do. I'll reenter Heaven with the souls of the just whom I have redeemed from Hell and shall be greeted by Your smile. There will be no anger, then, between You and the sons of men, only peace and reconciliation."

(Lines 266-343) The rest of the heavenly host gaze at the Son in admiration, waiting to see what His offer will mean. God accepts the Son's sacrifice, saying that His offer is the only means by which men could be saved. He, Himself, loves men enough to give up to them for a time His only Son. The Son will be born of a Virgin and will live on earth as a man. He will take Adam's place as the head of the human race, even though He will be Adam's son. Just as all men will die in Adam, so all men who choose to live in Christ will be saved. Thus, "heavenly love shall outdo hellish hate," and man will be redeemed. Nor will taking on man's nature lessen the Son's glory. Rather, His glory will be increased. He is God's only begotten Son, but His generous act means that He will hold His place in Heaven even more by merit than He does by right of birth. His humility will exalt His human nature, too, so that He will reign at God's right hand in the fullness of both His natures, as both God and man. All creation shall bow to the Son, in Heaven, on earth, and in Hell. At the end of the world, it is the Son Who will judge the dead who have been awakened from their sleep. The doors of Hell will be shut forever on the damned, and the just will dwell in a new World that will spring from the ashes of the old. When that time comes, the Son will no longer need His royal sceptre, for all of the blessed will be united in God's will. God ends His speech by commanding the angels to adore the Son, Who has accepted death in order that the glorious reign of truth may come to be.

(Lines 344-415) The angels rejoice at God's words and offer homage freely to both the Father and the Son, casting down their own crowns of gold. They take up their harps and sing with beautiful harmony hymns of praise to God's infinite glory. They praise the Son for having defeated Satan and his host when the fallen angels rebelled. They praise Him even more because His generosity will permit the Father to be merciful to men.

SATAN'S VISIONS:

(Lines 416-497) Meanwhile Satan has alighted on the margin of
the cosmos, the borderland between our world and chaos. It is still
dark and stormy where he stands, though in the distance he can
see the lights of Heaven. The world, which at first seemed to be
only a small globe, is now in his eyes a vast continent. The area
he treads is empty, but Milton says that it will thereafter be full
enough, for it is Limbo or the Paradise of Fools. The builders of
the Tower of Babel will be there. So will the Greek, Empedocles,
who sought to prove he was a god by jumping into the volcano,
Mount Aetna. It will hold all half-formed things, all monsters that
do not achieve full birth. Milton's objections, as a Puritan, to Roman
Catholicism show most sardonically when he couples "embryos and
idiots" with "eremites and friars." (Eremites are hermits.) Those
who go on pilgrimages to Jerusalem or to Rome or to other places
deemed holy in order to find salvation will dwell in Limbo. So will
those who thought to gain Heaven by dying in the robes of one of
the Catholic Church's religious orders. As these "fools" approach
St. Peter's gate after death, confidently expecting to be admitted,
they will be caught in a crosswind and blown instead into Limbo.

(Lines 498-612) The Fiend, or Satan, wanders across this dark
area until a gleam of light attracts his attention. He hurries toward
the light and sees that it comes from a magnificent golden staircase
ascending into Heaven. At its top is a gate embellished with dia-
monds and gold. The stairs are the ladder Jacob saw in a story told
in the *Book of Genesis*. The stairs, Milton says, are not always in
place. They can be drawn up into Heaven. They are down now,
either to dare Satan to try to reenter Heaven or to remind him of
his permanent exclusion from the City of God. Right next to the
gates, which open from beneath directly over Paradise where Adam
and Eve are living, is a passageway between Heaven and earth. It
is wide, wider than it has ever been since the Fall, permitting the
angels to go easily on God's business with men. Satan from the lowest of the stairs gazes upon the world in wonder, and even more in
envy, for God's newest creation is beautiful indeed. He drops in
flight past the stars in the firmament—not even pausing to see if
they are inhabited. He makes his way directly toward the sun, which
dominates the skies as God dominates Heaven. Satan lands on the
sun, which is inexpressibly brighter than anything that can be seen
on earth, far richer in gems and gold than is the earth.

(Lines 613-653) The Devil eyes the sun's beauty undazzled. Since
the sun is the center of light, no shadows impede his vision. Through
the perfectly clear air, he soon discerns, at a distance, Uriel. He is

the angel whom St. John describes in the *Book of Revelations* or
of the Apocalypse, the last book of the Bible. Uriel has his back to
Satan and seems to be absorbed either in thought or in fulfilling one
of God's commands. Satan rejoices to find someone who will perhaps direct him to Paradise. Before he approaches Uriel, however,
he assumes the shape of a youthful Cherub, a rank of angels con-
siderably below the Archangels, to which rank Satan had belonged
before his fall. Uriel hears Satan approaching and turns toward him.

(Lines 654-693) Satan, in disguise, addresses Uriel, referring to
him as one of the seven messengers who stand in readiness nearest
to God's throne. He tells Uriel that he has come from the ranks of
the Cherubim to look upon God's latest work—man. For to contemplate God's wonderful works is to discover new reasons for
praising Him. Even Uriel, the "sharpest-sighted Spirit of all in
Heaven," is fooled temporarily by Satan's hypocrisy. The innocent
—simply because they are innocent—do not expect others to practice deceit. Uriel replies to Satan:

(Lines 694-742) "Your desire to know God's works at first hand,
instead of simply relying on reports current in Heaven, merits
praise. But what created mind can grasp God's infinite wisdom and
power? I saw His Word bring order and light to Chaos and create
the world you see. Look down upon the globe below which shines
with light reflected from this sun. It is the Earth, the seat of Man.
I am pointing directly to Paradise, Adam's home. You cannot miss
your way, nor may I neglect mine."

Uriel turns away, and Satan, after bowing to him, as a Cherub in
Heaven would bow to an Archangel, takes flight toward Earth. He
lands upon Niphates, a mountain just to the north of Paradise.

COMMENT: The meeting in Heaven, which is the first episode
of Book III, is obviously intended to parallel the Satanic Consult in Book II. It is a meeting in which the forces opposed to
Satan determine strategy, just as Satan's host did. Furthermore,
the Son, after a proposal is greeted by the rest of the meeting
in awed silence, volunteers for a difficult mission, just as Satan
did. The similarity, however, serves to point up significant dif-
ferences, too. Only the principal devils attended the meeting in
Hell. The whole of the heavenly host is present at God's meeting. None of the manipulation Satan practiced is necessary.
God states His own case. He has no need to plant a stooge.
When He asks for a volunteer to accept death in order that men
may live, it is not necessary to call an abrupt halt to the meeting

after the Son volunteers. No one in Heaven would attempt to steal the Son's glory. Satan may think that there is envy in Heaven—as he said in his first long speech in Book II, but now that he is gone from those starry regions, envy is gone, too. It has followed him into Hell.

The Justification of God's Ways to Men: In Book I, Milton announced that the principal theme of his poem was "to justify the ways of God to men." It is in Book III that the justification is stated. First of all, God is not responsible for the fall of either the angels or of men. He has given them the gift of free will. He has told them what they must do and offered them the grace that will enable them to fulfill His commands. The danger of free will is that one who is free to choose is free to choose badly. Yet to deny so great a gift to His creatures would surely be less generous on God's part than to grant them free will, even though He knows that it will be abused.

Nor, says God, does His foreknowledge of sin make Him responsible for that sin. His knowledge is not the cause of the sin. The cause of the sin is the pride of both men and angels. If it seems that God is not being quite fair in this matter, consider the case of the teacher who knows very early in the term that a certain not very bright student will fail the course. The student does not know the material, and his inattentiveness in class and his negligence about homework mean he never will know it. Surely it is not the teacher's knowledge that causes the "F." It is the student's laziness.

Or look at the problem from another point of view. God is all-knowing because He is eternal. Instead of seeing events in time, He sees them all at once. Hence, the future, which is unknown to us simply because it is the future, is part of an eternal present to Him. If you are standing on a cliff overlooking a river, you can see a much larger stretch of the river than anyone standing on its banks. Thus, you will know that a canoe is on its way up the river long before a man on its shore will. Yet your knowledge does not cause the canoe to come. God sees the whole stream of human life from the vantage-point of a very high cliff, yet His knowledge is not the cause of its events.

The "Happy Fault":   God, then, is not to blame for man's sin and its consequences. Yet that fact justifies God only negatively. If God does no more for man, Satan will have won. He will have perverted or destroyed God's works. Hence, the more important part of God's justification comes in His offer of mercy to men. It is God's mercy that turns aside Satan's venom, that rescues men from his malice. Furthermore, Satan's malice leads to the generosity of the Son, who volunteers to be born as Jesus Christ and to accept man's punishment in order that men may be saved. Good, in other words, is brought out of Satan's evil. Traditionally Christians have been so much aware of that fact that they have referred to Adam's fall—the evil Satan is intent upon causing—as the *Felix Culpa,* the "happy fault," because if Adam had never fallen, Christ would never have been born. Thus, in the Son's act, as God says, "Heavenly love shall outdo hellish hate."

Man's redemption is the most obvious way in which good comes out of Satan's evil, thus justifying God's ways to men. But the possibility that good can come out of evil if men cooperate with God appears in the poem in other ways, too. For instance, Milton's prayer to Light—which is, incidentally, one of the traditional names for the Holy Ghost—is not just a touching plea from a blind man. It is significantly related to the theme of the poem. Milton's blindness is an undeniable evil. Yet he asks that God help him turn it to a good. He cannot see the physical world. Therefore, with God's grace, His "Celestial Light," Milton asks to be allowed to see even better than others can—because he will approach it without distraction, the truth that can be seen only spiritually.

Satan: In Books I and II Satan has appeared only in his own form. And even though he has been presented as haggard, pain-worn, we have always been aware of his native majesty. In Book III Satan assumes his first disguise. Notice that he takes the form of a *lesser* angel, a Cherub, a rank of angel far below his own in dignity and glory. The step will assume greater significance as we watch Satan in Book IV.

PARADISE LOST—BOOK IV

(Lines 1-31) Milton wishes for a warning voice like the one that St. John, who wrote the *Book of the Apocalypse,* heard in Heaven. Perhaps such a voice could have protected Adam and Eve from the Fiend who has come to tempt them. Satan does not rejoice at the speed with which he has traveled to the earth nor at the evil he is planning. For the evil has already begun to recoil upon him. His thoughts are troubled. They remind him of the Hell that is within him, the Hell which he can no more leave than he can leave himself. His reawakened conscience reminds him of what he once was and of how much he has lost. It reminds him, furthermore, that the deed he is about to commit will only make matters worse. If he does more evil, he will have to suffer more pain. He looks sometimes toward Paradise, or Eden, and sometimes toward the blazing noonday sun as he meditates upon his plight. The speech that follows reflects the fact that Satan is divided against himself. Part of him acknowledges that he has done wrong. Note, for instance, how often he addresses himself in the second person.

SATAN'S COLLOQUY WITH HIMSELF:
(Lines 32-113) "I address you, O Sun," he begins, "who shine above the earth like its God. I add your name to the list of those I hate because you remind me of all I have lost. I surpassed you in glory until my pride and my ambition led me to destroy myself by warring against God. Oh, why did I do it? It was He Who gave me my glory. And to serve Him was not hard. All He asked was that I give Him the praise and thanks that were His by right.

"But all the good He did for me has been turned into evil. I felt myself to be so high that I didn't want to be subject to anyone, not even to God. And so I cast off that immense debt of gratitude, a debt I couldn't pay because my gratitude could never equal His generosity. I did not understand that when one recognizes that he owes thanks to another, he has already paid his debt. Gratitude, then, is no real burden. Perhaps if God had made me a lesser angel, I would have been content. I would not have had the glory that made me ambitious. But, after all, if some other angel, created higher than I, had decided to rebel, I probably would have gone right along with him. Other archangels, with as much glory as I had, have remained true to God.

"Why didn't you remain true?" he asks himself. "You had free will just as they did. Whom or what have you to blame for your fall?"

"Nothing," Satan is forced to reply to his conscience, "but the love God offered equally to all the angels. His love is cursed, as far as I'm concerned, then, for His love has brought me eternal woe. He might as well have hated me for all the good I'm getting out of His love."

"Nay, curse yourself, rather, since you chose to set your will against His," says Satan's more truthful self.

"Ah, I am miserable," he continues. "Wherever I go, I am in Hell. I am Hell myself. And all I can see before me is a Hell so deep that the one I'm in now looks like Heaven in comparison. Why, then, don't I repent? Isn't there any road that leads to pardon?" Satan asks as he contemplates his agony. None, he tells himself, except submission. His pride will not allow him to take that path. Furthermore, he is ashamed to tell those he has led into Hell that he is giving up. He has boasted too much and too loudly that he will overthrow the Almighty. "They little know," he adds, "how dearly I pay for my boast and for the honor that they offer me as their leader. The higher they raise me, the lower I truly fall."

"But what if I could repent?" he goes on. "If I were once again high in the ranks of Heaven, I would be tempted again to rebel. I would soon retract the submission I only pretended to make. Ease would make me forget the pain that led me to repent. I hate God too much to be truly reconciled to Him. My second fall would be even worse than my first, and I would be buying temporary ease at the price of even greater punishment. Besides, since God knows as well as I do that I can't really repent, He's no more likely to grant me pardon that I am to sue for it. I have, therefore, no hope. Let me look, then, upon Man and this new world created for him. Since I have no hope, I have no fear and no remorse. Henceforth, my only Good is Evil. By doing evil, I shall at least be able to divide God's empire. I will reign, perhaps, over more than half of that empire, as Man and this New World soon shall know."

HIS HYPOCRISY IS REVEALED:
(Lines 114-171) As Satan speaks, each passion he suffers shows on his face. Such changes demonstrate that he is not the Cherub he is pretending to be. Angels' faces are never distorted because their minds are always at peace. Like the hypocrite he is, Satan assumes once more a peaceful expression as soon as he becomes aware that the violence of his emotions has shown on his face. But he isn't quick enough to deceive Uriel, as he did in Book III, for that angel has watched his descent and observed his torment.

The Fiend proceeds to Eden. Paradise, which is in the eastern part of Eden, is at the top of a mountain whose rough sides make Paradise, or the Garden of Eden, almost unapproachable. The Garden is surrounded, too, by walls of living green from which Adam can view the lower reaches of his kingdom. Within the walls grow stately trees bearing delicious fruit. The sun shining upon them makes the region more colorful than the rainbow. Satan has breathed only pure air since entering the Cosmos, but the air in Paradise is even purer. The scene is so beautiful and the atmosphere so fragrant that anyone—except the despairing Satan—could be happy in Paradise.

(Lines 172-287) Satan, mounting the hill at the top of which is Paradise, is stopped by the thickness of the undergrowth. The only gate into Paradise is in its eastern wall, and Satan has approached the Garden from the west. He leaps, therefore, over the wall and enters Paradise like a wolf looking for a victim. He flies onto the Tree of Life, which is in the middle of the Garden, and sits there disguised as a cormorant, a greedy bird of prey like a vulture. He does not think of the life-giving virtue of the tree in which he sits. He is, rather, devising ways of bringing death into the world. As he looks down from the tree, he sees beneath him a panorama of all the beautiful things with which the world abounds. Next to the Tree of Life is the tree that is to bring death upon mankind: the Tree of the Knowledge of Good and Evil. Eden is watered by a river that divides itself into four main streams running over golden sands. There are groves of trees in Paradise and open fields on which flocks graze. All flowers grow there, "without thorn the rose." There are cool grottoes and gentle waterfalls. Choirs of birds sing. The breezes stir the leaves into gentle melody. Spring reigns perpetually. The Fiend sees all these delights, yet remains himself undelighted.

(Lines 288-357) The noblest creatures that he sees are Adam and Eve. They walk erect, and their freedom and nobility declare that they are truly made to be the images of God. Adam's greater height and his nobler brow proclaim him to be the higher of the two. Eve is gentle. Her hair falls freely in curls to her waist. It twines about her as the vine twines about a tree and suggests that her proper role is submission. Because they have not sinned, neither of the two needs to be ashamed. Thus, they walk naked in native pride and innocence. They walk hand in hand, he the handsomest of men and she the most beautiful of women who have ever lived. After having worked just enough to make rest sweet and to give them the appetite they need to make their food delightful, they sit down beside a fountain to eat their supper. About them play all the beasts of the earth who have, since the Fall, been wild and the foes of men. The lion, the elephant, the bear, and all the other animals do their best to entertain the pair. The sun is about to set, and many of the animals are preparing for rest. Satan watches the beautiful scene in speechless wonder, at first, and finally says to himself:

(Lines 358-410) "These two human beings are so beautiful, show so clearly the Divine Hand that made them that I could love them." Addressing them silently, he goes on to say, "Little do you know how soon all the delights you enjoy will vanish. You are happy now, but too ill protected to continue to be happy. The fence that guards your Heaven was not enough to keep me out, and I am your foe. I don't want to be your foe. Though I am myself unpitied, I could pity you, for you are lovely and forlorn. I want to form so close an alliance with you that either I shall live on earth with you or you will dwell with me in Hell. You probably won't like Hell as well as you like Paradise. But it is what God has given to me, and I give it freely to you. It is a far wider place than Paradise, and there will be room in it for all your offspring. I don't want to wrong you, since you've never in any way hurt me. But I must do evil to you to get even with God. And though your harmless innocence melts my heart, I have to conquer this world. Public policy demands that I do. Honor, empire, revenge require that I injure you, though, if I were not damned, I would hate to hurt you."

SATAN'S OBSERVATIONS: Satan, thus, like all other tyrants, says that the public good requires him to do the evil he is contemplating. He leaps from the Tree of Life and assumes different animal shapes as he tries to get as close to Adam and Eve as possible, for he wants to learn more about them and about their way of life. Finally he hears Adam say to Eve:

(Lines 411-439) "The God Who raised us from the dust and set us in this beautiful place, giving us power over all the things we see, must indeed be good. There is nothing He really needs from us. All He has asked us to do in return for what He has given us is to obey one rule. We are not to eat of the Tree of Knowledge, for if we do, we shall taste Death, which is apparently something very dreadful. Since we are given so much power and so much freedom, we cannot resent this single restriction. Let us, therefore, praise God and enjoy our pleasant job of tending this Garden. For even if the work we do were hard, I would like to do it, for I do it with you."

(Lines 440-504) Eve answers, "O you from whose flesh I was made and without whom I would have neither purpose nor guide in life, you are quite right. We owe all our praise and all our gratitude to

God. And I owe even more than you do, because I have you. Since you are superior to me, it is impossible for you to find anywhere a spouse who is your equal. I remember very well the day on which I first awoke. I found myself lying on a bed of flowers under a tree. I wondered where I was, who I was, where I had come from, and how. Not far from me was a brook that issues from a cave and empties into a still pond. I went to look in it. In my inexperience I thought it was another sky. When I looked into it, a shape appeared that startled me. I jumped back, and so did it. But I advanced again and found it shared all my looks and all my feelings. I gazed at it and would have been caught by a vain desire for my own image except that a voice warned me, saying that what I saw in the pool was only my own reflection. If I followed the voice, I would be led to someone in whose image I was made. We would love each other, and I would bear children and become the Mother of the human race. I followed until I saw you. You were fair and tall, but not so lovely nor so gentle as that smooth image I had seen in the pool. I turned away, but you followed me, calling me Eve and telling me that I was running away from the person who had given me his flesh and blood. You had lent me life, you said, in order that you might have me by your side. You took my hand gently, and I yielded. And in knowing you, I have discovered how much better manly grace is than beauty. I know now, too, that wisdom alone is truly fair." She and Adam embrace. The Devil turns away from them in envy and says:

HIS ENVY OF THEIR PARADISE:

(Lines 505-535) "These two enjoy a paradise in each other's arms more blissful than this garden in which they live. How the sight torments me! How I hate them when I think that I am thrust into Hell where there is no love, no satisfaction for the fierce desires we feel. But I've learned something very important. These two lovers are forbidden to eat of the Tree of Knowledge. Why should God envy them knowledge? Are they safe only in their ignorance? I'll excite in them a desire for more knowledge: God in His envy intends to keep them in a lowly state. Knowledge will make them gods. Aspiring to be gods, they'll taste that forbidden fruit, and die. But first I must investigate this garden even more carefully. Perhaps some wandering Spirit from Heaven will tell me whatever else I need to know. Live and enjoy yourselves while you can, O happy pair," he says, looking once more at Adam and Eve, "for your brief pleasures will be followed by endless pain."

(Lines 536-609) Satan turns scornfully but slyly away and begins his exploration of the Garden. Meanwhile the setting sun shines against the eastern gate of Paradise, a rock of alabaster reaching to the sky. It offers only one entrance from the earth, an entrance the archangel Gabriel is guarding. He is the chief of the angels sent by God to guard Adam and Eve. The others, unarmed, are practicing heroic games, their armor hung high in readiness, should the need for it arise. Uriel comes hastily down from the sun to warn Gabriel that at noon that day one of the fallen angels, escaped from Hell, disguised as a Cherub, had asked the way to Eden. Uriel had discovered the hoax when he observed the devil's tortured countenance. The devil, though, is loose in Eden and must be found if Adam and Eve are to be protected. Gabriel tells him that no one without a right to enter the Garden has passed through the gate. If an evil spirit has leaped over the wall, however, he and his guards will have discovered him by dawn. Uriel returns to his post on the sun. Night falls over Eden, and the moon rises.

THE BLISSFULNESS OF LABOR:
(Lines 610-688) Adam tells Eve that it is time for them to go to bed. Their dignity as human beings requires that they work. Since they do, they grow tired sooner than the lesser animals who have nothing to do but roam aimlessly through the Garden. The two of them, he adds, must be up at sunrise if they are to have time to prune their plants and keep the paths they use free from unpleasant overgrowth. Eve agrees, telling him that it is her happiness to obey him. Nothing in the Garden, no matter how beautiful it may be, is pleasant unless she can be with him. She asks him then why the stars and moon are shining. Since they are about to go to sleep, nobody will be able to see their light. Adam tells her that they shine so that Old Night will never be able to regain his kingdom of total darkness. They move around the earth, as does the sun, providing light for people yet unborn who will live on the other side of the Earth. Besides, even though men sleep, millions of angels walk the Earth by both day and night, giving praise to God for the wonders of His creation. Doesn't she remember how often they have heard the spirits singing God's praises and have lifted their own minds to Heaven, too?

(Lines 689-775) The two go hand in hand to the lovely bower God has reserved for their use. No other animal ever enters it, since it is set apart for these two, who are the highest beings in the material world. They thank God for the day, the night, for their love, and for the children they will one day beget. Retiring to rest, they enjoy, in freedom and without shame, one another's love. Milton chooses this place to sing his praise of wedded love, of the joy and the order it imparts to human life. Adam and Eve are lulled sweetly to sleep by nightingales.

(Lines 776-796) At midnight when the guard of the Cherubim stands armed for the night watch, Gabriel speaks to Uzziel, his second-in-command, telling him to take half the troop along the edge of Paradise to the south, watching carefully for any enemy. He will lead the others to the north, and the meeting point for the two squadrons will be the western wall. As Uzziel's troops depart, Gabriel calls Ithuriel and Zephon—two angels close to him in rank —to him. He sends them to investigate the Garden itself. They are to search especially carefully the bower of Adam and Eve, for Gabriel has been told that one of the fallen angels has escaped from Hell and was seen winging his way toward Eden. If they find this evil spirit, they are to seize him and bring him to Gabriel.

(Lines 797-843) Gabriel leads his troops on their way, and Ithuriel and Zephon go straight to Adam's bower. They find Satan squatting like a toad at Eve's ear, trying to corrupt her fancy by an evil dream. At the touch of Ithuriel's spear, Satan is restored to his own shape and stands discovered. The two Cherubim are startled to behold his ugliness, but, unafraid, they ask him which of the hellish host he is. Satan tells them scornfully that if they don't recognize him, it shows that they are of small importance in Heaven. Everyone who was anyone knew him. Zephon answers, "Don't fool yourself into thinking that you still look as you did when you stood upright and pure in Heaven. Your glory has departed with your innocence. You are as ugly now as the sin you have committed. But come with us to our leader, to whom you must explain what you're doing here."

SATAN AGAIN REGRETS HIS LOSS:
(Lines 844-876) Satan is momentarily abashed by the Cherub's rebuke. He thinks once more of all that he has lost in losing goodness. He is most disconcerted to learn that his lustre and his glory have been so much diminished that he is no longer recognizable. But he speaks as scornfully as ever, saying that he would rather face the higher power, since in a battle with the leader he will either gain more glory or lose less. Zephon replies that Satan's fear means that he and his companion will be unable to discover how much of the devil's strength has been lost through wickedness. Satan is enraged, but curbing his anger, he goes with his captors to the western point where the two squadrons of angels have just met. Gabriel hears their approach and, as the three draw nearer, recognizes Satan. He warns his followers that Satan's angry scowl means that there will

probably be a fight. Ithuriel and Zephon bring their prisoner to Gabriel and present a complete report of his capture.

GABRIEL'S CHALLENGE TO SATAN:
(Lines 877-901) Gabriel asks Satan why he has come into the Garden and why he sought to disturb the sleep of Adam and Eve. His place is Hell, and he has no proper business in Paradise. Satan replies, "That's a rather foolish question, Gabriel, for one who has the reputation of being pretty smart. No one loves his pain. Had you been put in Hell, I'm sure you would have done your best to get out, too. I came here looking for comfort. If God intends us to stay in Hell, he'd better guard us more securely. It's true that your lieutenants found me near Adam and Eve, but that doesn't mean I intended any harm."

(Lines 902-923) Says Gabriel, "Who are you to tell anyone he's foolish, since you were foolish enough to lose Heaven? Nor have you learned yet what little you can gain by making God angry. Don't you know that your escape from Hell against God's will can only make your ultimate punishment worse? Besides, why are you the only one who has left Hell to escape its pains? Why aren't all your followers here, too, if that cowardly reason for your flight is true? You must have told *them* a different story!"

(Lines 924-945) Satan answers with a frown, "How dare you call my courage into question when you saw how I faced God's thunder, without which your spear would have accomplished little when we battled not so long ago in Heaven? All your questions show that you don't really know what you're talking about. A faithful leader —like me—faces first the dangers into which he intends to bring his followers. I've come alone from Hell to spy out this New World. I wanted to find out if I could settle my troops here or in mid air. And in order to possess this territory, we're ready to fight again. We're willing to see how much your legions, those angels who chose the easier path of obedience, are willing to suffer. They're cut out more for cringing in the distance and singing hymns than for fighting battles."

(Lines 946-967) Gabriel replies, "You keep shifting ground. First you pretended you'd left Hell to escape pain. Now you say you've come as a spy. Such answers suggest you're not a leader but a liar. How dare you call yourself faithful? Were you faithful to the rebellious crew you misled? Did faith suggest you should break your military vows of obedience to God? Hypocrite! You call yourself a patron of liberty, you who once fawned upon and cringed before

God! You thought you could dispossess Him if you hid your thoughts. But listen to my warning. Get back where you came from. If I find you here within the next hour, I'll drag you back to Hell in chains and seal you so tightly that you'll never again say Hell is too lightly barred!"

(Lines 968-1015) Satan, ignoring Gabriel's threats, shouts in rage, "Talk of chains when I'm your captive. But in the meantime expect to suffer even if the King whose chariot you so ignominiously draw assists you." As he speaks, Gabriel's troops mass for battle. Satan collects all his might and seems tall enough to reach the sky. A destructive battle might have taken place, but God, to prevent it, holds up His golden scales. When Gabriel sees the sign, he says to Satan: "Why do we stand here boasting? Both of us know that we can do no more than Heaven permits us to do. Read your fortune in that celestial sign. You are weighed in the balance, and you can see how weak and foolish your resistance will be." Satan, looking up, recognizes his destiny. He flies murmuring away, and "with him fled the shades of Night."

> **COMMENT:** It is in Book IV that Satan's character demonstrates most graphically Milton's understanding of the psychology of sin. Satan, created by God, possesses a nature which recognizes the truth and longs for the good. Thus, when he does evil, he does violence, first of all, to his own nature. As a matter of fact, he acts against himself to so great a degree that in parts of Book IV he seems almost to have a split personality.
>
> Notice particularly the long soliloquy that opens Book IV. It is Satan's moment of truth. In Book I he told the other devils:
>
> > The mind is its own place, and in itself
> > Can make a Heaven of Hell, a Hell of Heaven.
>
> Now he shows that he is aware of how bitterly true those lines are. "Which way I fly is Hell; myself am Hell." Having chosen to do evil, he cannot escape Hell, for the reality of Hell is in his tormented mind—just as he had said it would be. He may be about to enter Paradise, but it can be no Paradise for him.
>
> In the course of the soliloquy, Satan confirms much that God has said in Book III. Satan chose evil freely. He could have been true to God, had he wanted to be. The service God asked of him was mild. He is forced to acknowledge the whole of his folly in rebelling against God. He admits, as he never has before

in the poem, that God loved him, and that he has sinned against that love utterly without reason. It is at this point in the speech that Satan begins addressing himself in the second person. One part of him, clinging to the truth, recognizes his sin. The other parts insists upon loving that sin. There can be no real reconciliation between these two aspects of his personality, unless there can be a reconciliation between himself and God.

But there can be no such reconciliation simply because Satan will not submit. Since he will not repent, turn away from his sin, he cannot be forgiven. How, then, is he to give himself any peace? He tries to do so by destroying everything in himself that is good. At the beginning of his speech, he tells the sun he hates it. Why? In the light of the sun he cannot help seeing the truth. Since he has turned away from the truth, any reminder of it brings him only pain. At the end of the speech, when he has persuaded himself that his only Good is Evil, he has at least temporarily silenced his conscience, that aspect of himself which draws him to the truth. In the rest of the poem, we watch Satan destroy as completely as possible any vestige of the noble figure he once was. The irony of his self-destructiveness is that it is a road that will not give him the peace he seeks. He succeeds only in making himself unhappier than ever.

When he first sees Adam and Eve, he is as much attracted to them as he was repelled by Sin and Death when he met them at the gates of Hell. But he perverts his love for them. He persuades himself first that the only reason he is going to try to capture them is that he loves them. He loves them so much he wants them to be close to him, even if the closeness means only pain for them. And at the end of that speech, he justifies the wanton evil he intends these lovely and harmless creatures by saying that their suffering will be in "the public good."

He speaks of them again when he has observed their love for each other. Remembering that it is his lot to be coupled forever with hideous Sin, he allows his envy of their love to outweigh entirely any pity or gentleness their attractiveness has roused in him. In other words, he makes himself hate what his nature says he should love. And in doing so, he necessarily does violence to that nature.

Satan's Disguises: Satan's self-destructiveness is symbolized by the shapes he assumes. At the end of Book III, he disguised himself as a Cherub, a lesser angel. After he has leapt into the

Garden, he sits on the Tree of Life in the shape of a cormorant. He has become an animal, but one, at least, who can soar through the air with some of the freedom that belongs to the angels. To observe Adam and Eve more closely, he takes the shape of a lion and then of a tiger. These four-footed creatures are limited to movement upon the earth, but they can run, and men usually think of them as noble, even though they are dangerous. When Satan whispers in Eve's ear as she sleeps, he has reduced himself to a toad, an animal that crawls along the surface of the earth and is, to most people, much nastier than it is dangerous. Note the progression: Archangel to Cherub to bird to beast to toad. Each change brings him nearer the earth, lower in the spiritual scale than he was before.

The result of his physical and moral change appears with dramatic effect when he is forcibly returned to his own person by Zephon's sword. Satan thinks his actions have no effect upon his personal glory. He does not realize that when he chooses to be a toad, he makes it impossible for himself ever to be an Archangel again. He is stunned by the discovery of his own ugliness.

Satan and Truth: Book IV corrects, as does the rest of the poem, the facts that Satan has distorted. He is given to bragging about his courage, his sincerity, the way in which he always stood up fearlessly for his rights. The picture of the noble rebel becomes a bit tarnished when we realize that Satan is always sly. After having voiced the venomous envy the love between Adam and Eve has roused in him, he turns scornfully away, but "with sly circumspection." And Gabriel tells us that Satan, as he plotted his rebellion, was also sly. He did not speak out boldly, as he would have us think; he cringed and fawned upon God, hoping to fool Him.

In his exchange with Gabriel, we hear Satan say the kind of thing a juvenile delinquent might say. He says that those who remained true to God remained true because obedience was the easier, the cowardly path. Thus does one nine-year-old taunt another nine-year-old into smoking: "You'll be a sissy if you don't!"

It is interesting to note, too, that Satan, like most sinners, sees his besetting sin everywhere. He is obsessed with envy. Because he is, he can see God's prohibition to Adam and Eve as an act of envy, too. He is, by the time he hears of the law, so much possessed by evil that, in spite of his natural intelligence, he cannot see at all what the restriction really means, a question we will consider in a moment.

Paradise: Milton's representation of Paradise is touchingly beautiful, but somehow doomed. We are constantly reminded that Adam and Eve will not enjoy its peace for long. First of all, there is Satan's presence. Secondly, the Tree of Life stands next to the Tree of the Knowledge of Good and Evil, and we are never allowed to forget what that tree stands for. More subtly, the beasts that are mentioned as friendly to Adam and Eve are those that are most unfriendly now—tigers, lions, leopards, etc. And at the end of the idyllic scene in which the animals seek to amuse the human pair, we see the wily serpent, whose shape Satan will assume when he tempts Adam and Eve. Every statement of the sweetness of life in Paradise, then, tends to remind us of the conditions in which we live now. When Milton says that in Paradise one found "without thorn the rose," how can we help but think of the thorns we encounter now?

Adam and Eve: There is foreshadowing, too, in the depiction of Adam and Eve. Adam's first speech is about the restriction God has imposed upon them. What he is saying is that he has no intention of breaking that rule. But one way in which to be tempted to break rules is to think too much about them. Since the two are nowhere near the tree, if the speech reveals anything at all about Adam, it suggests that the tree is a little too much on his mind.

The foreshadowing in relationship to Eve is much more clearly evident. When she tells about the first day of her life, she tells the reader, also, about the weak point in her character: vanity. She nearly fell in love with her own image in the pond. She is saved from that fatal narcissism by God's voice. But the incident serves also to remind us that she can be swayed by vanity.

The Tree of Knowledge: The position of Adam and Eve in Paradise is very like that of Satan before his fall. Satan was the highest of angels, needing to obey only God and His Son. Adam is the highest creature on earth, needing to obey only God. His obedience takes a specific form: he must not eat of the fruit of the Tree of the Knowledge of Good and Evil. Satan thinks God has made the restriction out of envy. But since Satan—as he himself admits in his long speech at the beginning of Book IV —misunderstood his own obligations in Heaven, perhaps he misunderstands Adam's, too.

First of all, the restriction is not against knowledge as such, for Adam, as we shall see later, is encouraged to know. The tree concerns a particular knowledge: the knowledge of good and evil. How does one come to know the difference between good and evil? Satan, in the poem, demonstrates how. No one can know evil so well as he, nor can anyone else know so well how much it differs from good. And his knowledge, as we know, comes from the fact that he has *done* evil. The restriction, then, understood in the light of Satan's experience—and of the experience of most human beings, too, means simply that God has commanded Adam and Eve to *do* no evil. They are not to want the kind of knowledge they can have only through sin. And when we see what the consequences of such knowledge have been for Satan, we realize that it is not an enviable knowledge at all.

PARADISE LOST—BOOK V

(Lines 1-94) Adam awakes with the first hint of dawn and is surprised to discover that Eve is still asleep. She looks, too, as though her rest has been a disturbed one. He calls to her in a gentle whisper. She wakes up and, embracing Adam, says that she is glad to look again upon him and on the morning. For she had had an evil dream. "I heard a voice I thought was yours asking why I slept when all Heaven was awake and longing for the sight of me. When I arose, I could not see you. I walked about looking for you and found myself at the Tree of Knowledge. It seemed much more tempting than it does by day. Near it stood someone who looked like an angel. He, too, gazed at the tree, saying what a pity it was that no one ate its beautiful fruit. Did everyone despise knowledge? Was it out of envy that we were forbidden to eat it? At any rate, *he* would eat the fruit. To my horror, he did. And when he had, he offered some to me, saying that the fruit was capable of making gods of men. He told me that if I ate the fruit, I would live a goddess among gods. When he held a piece of the fruit close to my mouth, it was so tempting that I ate it. And then I flew with him to the clouds and looked down in wonder upon the Earth. My guide disappeared, and I sank down to sleep. But I'm so glad the whole thing was only a dream!"

(Lines 95-208) Adam says that anything that troubles Eve troubles him, too, particularly this dream, which seems to be an evil one.

But the evil cannot have come from Eve, for she is good. It must be that her fancy, freed from the control of her sleeping reason, had put together the events of the preceding day in a grotesque, disordered fashion. The dream did contain fragments of their evening's conversation. But something new and frightening was added: Eve succumbed to the temptation of the Tree. However, evil can come into the mind of man without his consent. And since Eve is so much upset at the notion of transgressing God's law even in a dream, she certainly will never do it in reality. "Therefore," he adds, "be cheerful, as you usually are, and let us enjoy our morning's work." She dries two tears, and he kisses away two others.

GOD PRAISED THROUGH WORKS: They go outside and pause to say their morning prayers before they begin the day's work. "We know You, O God, only through these, the least of your works," they say. "Since they are so beautiful, how much more beautiful You must be. O angels, praise God, for, since you can see Him, you can do it far better than we can. O stars and sun and moon, praise Him, for it is He Who brought light out of darkness. The air, the elements, the wind should praise Him, as should the plants and the waters. And all living things, the birds and beasts of the air, the water, and the earth, should join us now in praising Him. O Lord, if any evil has come near us in the night, send it away with the coming of the day."

(Lines 209-307) Their peace restored, they hurry to do their pleasant work. God looks down upon them in pity. He says to Raphael, the "sociable spirit": "You know what Satan has been doing in the Garden. I want you to go to talk to Adam as a friend. Tell him his happiness depends upon his own free will. Warn him that Satan is plotting his downfall, not by violence but by deceit. Tell him so that when he sins, he will not be able to say that he was caught unaware." Raphael departs immediately on his errand. The gate of Heaven opens for him, and beneath him he sees Eden. He wings his way like the Phoenix—a mythological bird that was said to rise again from its own ashes—through the skies and lands in Paradise. He resumes his proper shape. He is a six-winged Seraph. The bands of angels whose business it is to guard Eden recognize him and bow to him, for they know he comes as God's messenger. He passes their tents and goes through the beautiful forests of Paradise.

From the door of his bower, where he has been resting from the noonday sun, Adam sees Raphael coming. He calls to Eve, who is preparing lunch:

(Lines 308-349) "Come see the glorious angel who is coming to-ward us. Perhaps he brings us a message from Heaven. If so, he may consent to be our guest. Hurry, then, and see what beautiful fruits we can serve him from our store." Eve replies that there is little need to store food when they enjoy so plentiful a supply, but she will find the choicest fruits the trees provide so that their guest will know that God has been as generous on earth as He is in Heaven. She hurries out, carefully planning her meal so that each food she serves will complement the rest. She prepares both food and drink and strews the ground with roses and other sweet-smelling shrubs.

(Lines 350-460) Adam goes without pomp in his native dignity to meet the angel. He bows to Raphael, as befits the angel's higher rank, and invites his guest to enjoy the coolness of his bower and to taste the best of the food he has to offer. Raphael accepts his offer, and when the angel reaches their bower, he greets the lovely Eve with "Hail," the salutation that will later be addressed to Mary. The three of them sit near a grassy mound, which will serve as their table. They converse pleasantly and then Adam invites Raphael to eat, though he is doubtful about whether or not the food he has to offer is suitable for angels. Raphael assures him that it is and ex-plains that angels, like all created things, need food for their suste-nance. The food in Heaven is more sublime than what grows upon the Earth. But God has given the Earth such varied delights that Raphael will partake of Adam's meal with joy. The three eat heartily, and when they have finished, Adam says to Raphael:

(Lines 461-505) "I am grateful for the honor you have done me in condescending to eat these earthly fruits with me." Raphael explains that all things God had created are made of the same matter. Angels, as the beings nearest God, are the most refined, the purest, of God's creatures, but they differ from men only in degree, not in kind. It is, therefore, not surprising that he, an angel, can enjoy Adam's food, converting it, as he eats, into his own proper substance. A time may come when Adam, purified into a pure spirit, may eat angel's food and find it not too light to satisfy him. Such will be his fate if he is true to God's commands.

(Lines 506-518) Adam replies, "I understand well what you've said about our possible ascent to God. But why do you say that I will find this joy *if* I am obedient to God. Would it be possible for us to disobey the God Who has been so good to us?"

(Lines 519-560) Raphael, at last delivering the message he has been sent to give, tells Adam to thank God for the happiness he enjoys. He must remember, though, that it is up to him to keep that happiness by obedience. Adam has been made to be free. Nothing will compel him to be true to God, for God wants obedience freely given from men and angels. And some of the angels *have* failed to obey and have been plunged into the deepest Hell.

RAPHAEL'S STORY: Adam knows, he says, that he was created free, but he is quite sure that he will never disobey God. He is moved to doubt a little, though, at the news that some of the angels have fallen. It is just possible that he could fall, too. He asks Raphael to tell him more about that event.

(Lines 561-615) After a brief pause, Raphael begins his tale. "It is difficult for me to tell you these things, Adam, not only because it is painful to talk of those who were once perfect and are now ruined. It is hard, also, to make these spiritual events understandable to you whose knowledge comes through your senses. But I'll do my best to discover analogies that will make these matters plain to you. Before this world was created, God summoned all the angels of Heaven to His throne. When we had gathered in all our splendor, God, seated next to His Son, spoke to us. He declared that, from that day, the Son was to be our Head. 'I have anointed Him your King,' He said. 'You are to venerate Him and to obey Him. Live under His rule in unity. Anyone who disobeys Him, disobeys Me and will be cast out of Heaven into darkness for all eternity.'

(Lines 616-672) "Everyone seemed pleased with God's words," Raphael continues, "but not everyone was. All the angels spent the day dancing in praise of God. At evening they rested and ate, and finally dispersed for the night. Satan, however, neither retired to rest nor stayed in adoration at God's throne. He is called Satan now, for his former name is no longer spoken in Heaven. He was the highest of the archangels. He could not bear to think that the Son had been appointed King over Him, for it seemed a slight to his own glory. He had decided that when midnight came, he would depart with all his legions and would no longer obey God's commands. He awoke his second-in-command and said:

(Lines 673-710) " 'Can you sleep when you think of these new laws God has made? Since God makes new laws, we may react to them in new ways. However, it isn't safe to talk of these things here. Tell the leaders of our host that I am withdrawing to our homeland in the North. I want them to come with me so that we may plan a proper reception for our new King, the Messiah.' (The word means 'the anointed one.') His lieutenant did his bidding, phrasing commands in such a way that he could sound out the loyalty of those in Satan's legions and could taint their integrity as Satan had tainted his. All obeyed because Satan held such high power in Heaven. He succeeded in luring away one-third of Heaven's host.

(Lines 711-742) "God, of course, saw what Satan was doing. He turned, with a smile, to His Son, and said, 'We had better muster those forces left to us, for someone is planning to establish a rival kingdom in the North and even to overturn Our Throne. We don't want to be caught napping.' Said the Son, 'You're quite right to laugh at Your foes. Their attempt is vain. All that it will accomplish is to give Me an opportunity to show the power that You have given Me when I subdue them.' "

SATAN'S DECEPTIONS:

(Lines 743-802)   Meanwhile Satan and his host had flown into the North. He called his legions together before his throne to consult, he said, about their reception for the King. He spoke to them falsely and trickily, as follows: 'Thrones, Dominations, Princedoms, Virtues, Powers—these titles may be merely titles now, since the Son has usurped all the authority for which they once stood. He is called now the King Anointed, and we are to adore Him as we adore the Father, to adore Two, when adoring One seemed to be more than enough. Perhaps I've called you on this hasty midnight march to plan a reception for Him, to see how we can best bow down before Him. But maybe there is a way, instead, to cast off this yoke. We are all equally free, even though we are not equal in power. How can anyone ask us to serve when we have been ordained to govern?'

(Lines 803-852) "Satan had it all his own way, until Abdiel, one of the Seraphim, said: 'How can you, Satan, for whom God has done so much, dispute His word? As our Creator, hasn't He the right to tell us Whom we are to obey? And can you declare yourself equal to His Son, to the Word by Whom you and the rest of us were created? By making the Son our Head, God does not reduce our glory. He permits us rather to share in the Son's, and through the Son, in His own. Stop trying to seduce your followers, and make your peace with the Father and the Son while there is still time.'

"But no one had the sense to pay heed to Abdiel, and Satan's next words were even more arrogant than his first had been:

(Lines 853-876) " 'You say that we were made by God, that, furthermore, He transferred that task to the Son. Can anyone remember this creation? We know of no time when we were not. Were we not, then, self-created? Our power is our own, and we'll test it against the Almighty. Carry this message, Abdiel, to the Anointed King, and do it quickly before we intercept your flight!' The others murmured their approval of his words. Abdiel, alone, answered him:

(Lines 877-907) " 'I see that you are determined to fall and that all of your followers are caught in this fraud. You'll no longer need to worry about the Messiah's gentle yoke. A harsher law has been decreed for you. I shall take your advice and go, but not because I fear you. God's thunder will light upon you soon. You'll learn the hard way Who created you when you discover that He can *uncreate* you, too!'

"Thus spoke Abdiel, the only one of all that host who was loyal to the truth. He departed, not in fear, but because he scorned those who were false."

COMMENT: Eve's dream is another device Milton uses to foreshadow the coming Fall. It explains the effects of the Devil's attempt to corrupt her while she slept. It also presents a preview of her temptation scene. Note the appeal to her vanity, as Satan tells her she is the creature for whom all the stars are shining and for whom all the heavenly beings are waiting.

After the morning prayer of Adam and Eve, God sends Raphael to warn them of their danger. When they fall, they will not be able to say that they were not forewarned. Events after the Fall will show that God's warning is indeed a kindness to Adam and Eve, even though it seems simply to increase their responsibility for their sin.

That the angels, according to Milton, have digestive systems may come as something of a surprise to many readers. Milton, in this section, is not following traditional Christian doctrine. He is philosophically a materialist. The term does not mean that he loved money the way Mammon does. Rather, it means that he believed all reality to be made of the same substance—matter. To Milton, such a theory made possible the communion between Adam and Raphael and meant that Adam by right living could rise to a higher state of being, just as in the material universe, dead matter rises to a higher state by becoming part of the substance of a living material thing. Perhaps such a doctrine was the only one that permitted him to rescue material reality from Puritanical contempt. It enabled him, also, to give back to man's body the dignity of which Puritanism tends to rob it.

Satan's Rebellion: Raphael's account of Satan's rebellion presents some new corrections of Satan's lies. He did not stand up boldly, as he has said, for freedom. The first shadow of sin that entered his mind made him hypocritical and sly. He pretended obedience to God's decree for a whole day and then sneaked away with his followers for fear of God's sudden reprisal. Nor did God tremble for His throne at Satan's threats, as Satan claimed in his speeches to his host in Hell. God and the Son greeted the news of the rebellion with derisive smiles, knowing that their power could easily put down the upstart.

The real hero of the scene is Abdiel, the one member of Satan's legions who has the integrity and the courage to stand up alone against error. He is Milton's own invention. Nothing is said about such a figure in any of Milton's possible sources. That Milton admired Abdiel is evident. Abdiel, furthermore, is very much what Satan would like to have us believe Satan is. Abdiel is truly bold, truly independent, indeed capable of exercising the freedom Satan so often talks about. He is completely free of the need to stand well before his fellows. He follows his conscience, not public opinion. Recall, in contrast, Satan's soliloquy at the beginning of Book IV. He admits that he is ashamed to repent, though he knows he should, because of what his followers will say. To be influenced by such a motive is to follow, not to lead. Abdiel's presence, then, serves to remind us of how very paltry Satan really is, in spite of the splendor of his rhetoric.

Satan's refusal to obey God leads him immediately into a logical absurdity as well as into hypocrisy. He claims to be "self-created." One need not believe in a God Who creates to recognize that such a position is impossible. To be able to create himself, Satan would have had to exist *before* he had been created, to be in existence before he was brought into existence—a situation that is clearly absurd.

The Relation of God and His Son: Milton is somewhat ambiguous in his presentation of the Blessed Trinity. Many commentators, particularly Denis Saurat, have thought that Milton did not believe in the Trinity at all. He believed, according to them, that God is a single person and that Christ is not really God become man, but rather a man whose singular virtue made him able to become God. Whether or not such an interpretation of Milton's thought is true, Milton is careful to voice doctrine largely in accordance with traditional Christian positions in *Paradise Lost*. Thus, when the Father in Book V declares that

He has this day "begotten" His Son, He does not mean that the Son had not existed before. Such a position would have been extremely heretical, for it would have denied any possibility of equality between the Father and the Son. The word "begotten" means, instead, that God is that day begetting His Son as King, declaring Him to be Messiah. The Son's prior existence is proved through Abdiel's statement that it was by means of the Son that the angels were created.

PARADISE LOST—BOOK VI

RAPHAEL DEVELOPS HIS STORY:

(Lines 1-55) Raphael, continuing his account of Satan's fall, says, "Abdiel hurried back, reaching God's citadel by morning, to discover that God and the faithful angels already knew of Satan's rebellion. Abdiel's friends brought him before the throne of God, Who praised him for suffering universal reproach in order to be loyal to the truth. God, then, told him to join the battle against Satan and sent out the host of faithful angels under Michael, the prince of Heaven's warriors, and Gabriel, who is our second greatest fighter. We were told to pursue Satan and his rebels and force them into Hell.

(Lines 56-130) "God's legions formed into squadrons and marched to the North, where they met Satan's host hurrying in an attempt to take God by surprise. We, who had been accustomed to meet one another only in love, met in furious battle. Satan moved with haughty steps to the front of the battle. When Abdiel saw him, he decided to attack Satan. For though the apostate looked as powerful as ever, Abdiel was sure that his faithlessness must have lessened his strength just as it had weakened his intelligence. They met between the battle lines, and Abdiel said:

(Lines 131-148) " 'You thought you would be unopposed in your attempt to dethrone God, that all of us would either join you or fly from you in terror. You fool! Don't you know, yet, that God could destroy you even without our aid? But, you see, many of us prefer loyalty to rebellion. Even though I stood alone against you last night, learn now that sometimes truth rests not with the thousands but with the few.'

(Lines 149-170) "Satan replied, 'Too bad for you that you who set yourself against a third part of the gods last night should meet me here today. I had thought that all the angels would have preferred freedom to slavery. But most of them are too lazy to rebel. We'll see, though, if these servile psalm-singers can stand up against those of us who fight to be free!'

(Lines 171-261) "Abdiel replied that those of us who serve God are truly free, for we are following nature. The devil's followers are the slaves. They are following one who is unworthy. For himself, he added, Abdiel 'would rather serve in Heaven than reign in Hell.' Then Abdiel struck Satan on the crest of his helmet with such force that the Apostate was forced back ten paces and fell to his knee. The battle between the whole of both forces was joined with such violence that all Heaven resounded with the noise. Each of the angels on either side fought as though the whole battle depended upon him. The fortunes on both sides hung in equal balance until Satan, who had that day shown unbelievable strength, saw that many of his host were falling beneath Michael's terrible sword. He hurried to interpose his shield of adamant to protect them. Michael was glad to have the chance to fight him, for the defeat of Satan would mean the end of the war.

(Lines 262-353) " 'Author of Evil,' shouted Michael, 'go down into Hell with your rebellious crew and trouble the peace of Heaven no more! Go, before I send you there with this sword or before God's vengeance topples you with even greater pain!' "

SATAN IS WOUNDED:　"Satan replied, 'Don't try to frighten me with threats. I'll fight on until I turn Heaven into this Hell you keep talking about, if I need to, in order to live here freely.' The two began their duel, as the other combatants cleared a spot for them. They seemed to be as mighty as gods when both of them raised their swords. Michael's sword, made so that nothing can resist it, wounded Satan, who for the first time knew pain. Angelic substance soon heals itself, however, and Satan's followers interposed their shields so that he could be carried from the field. He gnashed his teeth in rage and humiliation, for he had discovered that he was no match for Michael, much less for God.

(Lines 354-417) "Other deeds deserve mention, too," continues Raphael. "Gabriel forced Moloch to flee, and Uriel and Raphael vanquished Adramelech and Asmadai. (Adam does not know Raphael's name, and so Raphael modestly refers to himself in the third person instead of boasting of his deeds.) Abdiel fought valiantly, too. I could speak of countless others, but those who were true to God are contented with their fame in Heaven. Those who rebelled deserve only silence since they sought fame through deeds of infamy. When we had defeated the leaders of the Satanic host, our troops marched in close formation forcing backward their disordered ranks, until the coming of night imposed a truce. Michael's forces camped on the battlefield, and Satan withdrew his legions to hold a new consultation.

(Lines 418-445) "Satan addressed his troops with all of his old pride. 'We've discovered,' he said, 'that we can withstand the best that Heaven has to send against us. It's true that we have suffered wounds, and they have not, but what do wounds matter when we heal so rapidly and so completely? We'll win all we have set out to win. Let us see if we can discover new weapons that will make us equal or superior to our foes, that will outweigh the fact that they can wound us and we are unable to hurt them.'

(Lines 446-523) "The next speaker was Nisroch, the leader of the Principalities—one of the orders of angels—who had joined Satan. His arms completely destroyed, he spoke gloomily. 'O great Liberator, what good does our valor do us when we must fight in pain against those whom we cannot injure? The inventor who can discover either a new weapon or some new means of protection for us will surely deserve thanks as great as that we offer to you, our deliverer.'

"Satan replied that he had such an invention. 'Let us dig in the ground for explosives. We shall force these minerals into iron tubes, ignite them, and release upon the forces of Heaven such destruction that we shall soon overwhelm them. Cheer up. Get to work, and we shall have acquired our new weapons by dawn.' His troops discovered under the surface of Heaven the sulphur they needed. They made gunpowder and cannon, and by morning their secret weapon was ready.

(Lines 524-608) "When morning came, the Heavenly host assembled and sent out scouts to find the foe. Zophiel, the swiftest of the Cherubim, warned our forces to arm because Satan and his host were on their way, grim and determined. Michael's army marched forward and met Satan's. His troops were so arranged that our forces could not see his new weapon. Satan called to his troops, saying ambiguously that he would open his defenses and sue, quite loudly, for peace. At his words, his forces parted ranks and displayed three cannon. We stood bemused, not knowing what the devilish

engines were. We soon found out, for a Seraph lit each one. Soon
Heaven was covered with fire and smoke. We were routed, for we
could not stand against the rocks and thunder unleashed upon us.
Nor could we retreat in orderly fashion, for our armor impeded us.
We didn't know what to do. Any attempt to rush Satan's forces
would lead to a similar disaster, for we saw three other Seraphim
ready to fire the cannon once more. Satan, seeing our plight, shouted
to his followers:

(Lines 609-679) " 'What happens when we offer to expose our
front and compose terms of peace? Our foes seem to prefer to practice some strange kind of dance.' Belial answered in a similar vein
of humor, 'We offered them weighty terms that they couldn't understand. Our terms have the gift, it seems, of showing us when our
enemies can't walk upright.' " So the devils mocked, thinking they
could defeat God and His forces through their inventiveness because our forces stood for a time in trouble.

GOD'S INTERVENTION: "But we didn't stand that way for long.
Our fury made us inventive, too. We cast away our arms, for they
were useless. We hurried to the hills of Heaven and, plucking them
up, threw them with their rocks and woods and rivers upon the foe,
burying those devilish engines. Then we invaded their forces and
buried them, legions at a time, under the mountains we bore. Satan's
host, in imitation of us, uprooted hills near them, and all Heaven
would have been ruined, had not the Almighty Father intervened.
He had permitted the battle to rage because he wished it to be
an occasion for the Son to manifest His glory.

(Lines 680-745) "Said He to the Son, 'This fighting has gone on
for two days, and the forces are nearly equal. After all, both sides
are composed of angels. Though Satan's forces are weakened by
sin, the havoc wrought by evil has not yet progressed far enough
to make them easy to defeat. But the third day of the battle will be
Yours. Only You can end it. And the grace and power You hold
from Me will prove beyond doubt that You are King because You
deserve to be. Ride My chariot, and use all My arms to send these
Sons of Darkness into Hell!'

" 'To do Your bidding is My greatest joy,' the Son responded. 'I'll
force those who are Your enemies out of Heaven and when I return,
Heaven's Saints and I shall hymn Your praises in joy.'

(Lines 746-823) "Bowing, the Son arose, and on the third morning
of the battle, the Chariot of God rushed forth like the whirlwind,

drawn by four Cherubim. The Son ascended the chariot's sapphire throne and, attended by ten thousand thousand Saints (angels who had remained true to God) went forth to battle. Our forces saw Him first and rejoiced to see His emblem blaze across the sky. At His command, the mountains returned to their places. Nonetheless, the foe still insisted upon fighting. Messiah's glory was, for Satan's troops, only another reason for envy. The Son told our host to rest. We had fought well, but God, to Whom all vengeance belongs, had appointed Him to administer punishment to Satan and his forces. 'It is I they have despised, and it is I Who will pour out upon them God's punishment.'

(Lines 824-892) "The Son's countenance became terrifying, full of wrath against His enemies. He rode His chariot into Satan's hordes and flung thunder and lightning at them. Astonished, they ceased to resist and dropped their idle weapons. The Son's lightning and His arrows seared them with fire, made them long for the cover of the mountains they had feared. But Messiah withheld half His strength, for He did not intend to destroy Satan, only to force Him out of Heaven. He lifted up His foes, when they had fallen, and drove them' like a herd of goats to Heaven's crystal wall. That opened wide and revealed the Deep, a sight so horrible the defeated fell back when they beheld it. But they had no choice. The Son forced them into Chaos down to the bottomless pit. Hell, itself, would have fled in fright from the noise and confusion, but Fate decreed that it could not. Nine days Satan and his host fell through Chaos until at last Hell closed its gates upon them. Heaven rejoiced to be rid of them, and soon repaired the wall. Messiah returned in triumph and was escorted by the cheering Saints to the throne of God, where He sits now at God's right hand.

(Lines 893-912) "Thus," concludes Raphael, "I have tried to tell you about these Heavenly events which otherwise you couldn't have known. For I want you to learn from Satan's example. He envies you your happiness and wants to seduce you into his company to spite the God he disobeyed. He might have stood, but he fell. Because you can fall, too, heed my warning. Tell Eve, too. And don't yield to the temptation he will offer."

COMMENT: The events of Book VI, which presents Satan's defeat and Messiah's triumph, are clear enough to require little comment.

Note that Abdiel is once again contrasted to Satan. Not only does he strike the first blow against the Apostate, but also the words he uses echo Satan's. Satan, in Book I, had said (ll. 264)—"Better to reign in Hell than serve in Heaven." In his answer to Satan's challenge in Book VI, Abdiel says (ll. 183-184):

Reign thou in Hell, thy kingdom; let me serve
In Heaven God ever blest.

That Milton deliberately recalls Satan's words suggests, again, that he wishes the reader to see Abdiel as the hero Satan intends himself to be.

PARADISE LOST—BOOK VII

(Lines 1-39) Milton calls upon Urania, the name given by the ancient Greeks to the muse of Astronomy. But he is calling not upon the ancient muse, but rather upon what that name stood for: heavenly inspiration. For such inspiration was born, not on Mount Olympus, as the Greeks thought, but in Heaven itself. He has sung of Heaven in the last two books. He wants help now to return successfully to the safer region of Earth to finish his task. He sings still, even though he sings in darkness amid the dangers of the evil days in which he lives. But as long as inspiration comes to him, he is not truly alone. He asks that Urania continue to govern his song and help to direct it to the sober, serious few who can read it with profit.

ADAM'S QUEST FOR KNOWLEDGE:
(Lines 40-110) Adam and Eve have listened to Raphael's story with wonder. When Raphael has finished, Adam seeks knowledge about the world in which he lives, saying to his guest: "We thank you, and we thank God for sending you to warn us of our danger. We will heed your warning, too. Can you then tell us how this world was made and why our great Creator decided to make it? We want to know about it not for any vain reason but so that, understanding more about God's works, we can praise Him more." Raphael replies:

(Lines 111-173) "Since you've asked so modestly, I shall be glad to grant your request. I'll do my best to tell you, since I was commissioned to answer all the questions you ask about what you have a right to understand. Beyond those bounds, do not go, and don't be tempted to make up explanations for the things you don't understand. Knowledge, like food, must be taken in moderation."

"After Satan had been driven into Hell," Raphael begins, "God said to His Son, 'Satan has failed to dethrone Us. And though he tempted many into folly, enough remain true to Us to people Heaven. However, so that Satan cannot boast that any places in Heaven are forever vacant, I shall create a new race of men who will live on a new world—Earth. By right living they will unite Heaven and Earth, and we shall all live together in peace and joy. I shall perform this work by Thee, My Son. I send You forth, together with the Holy Spirit, to make Heaven and Earth out of Chaos.' (Note that Heaven can mean both God's dwelling place and the heavens, or the sky.)

(Lines 174-242) "The Son set forth immediately to fulfill the Father's word. The heavenly choir sang hymns in praise of God Who brought forth good out of evil. For to replace the evil angels, He created a new world and a new race to serve Him better and to diffuse His goodness throughout the ages. The Son, meanwhile, in glory in His chariot, surrounded by an honor guard of angels, went through the gates of Heaven and looked out upon the Sea of Chaos. He silenced the angry waves and rode down into the heart of Chaos. He used golden compasses to measure off the limits of the universe and then hung the Earth in balance on her golden chain.

RAPHAEL'S STORY OF CREATION:
(Lines 243-338) " 'Let there be light,' He said, and there was light. God divided the night from the day. So ended the first day, amid the hymns of the angels. On the second day, God made the Firmament to separate the waters that are above the world from those that are below. The Earth had been formed already, but it lay yet, an embryo, in the womb of the Ocean, which imparted to the new globe life-giving power. Then God gathered the waters into one place so that dry land could appear. He called the waters Sea, and the dry land He named Earth. He saw that all that He had done was good, and He called upon the Earth to bring forth living grass and plants and trees of all kinds and of all colors. And when the Earth had burst into bloom and into life, it seemed almost like Heaven. And so ended the third day.

(Lines 339-449) "Then God made the sun and the moon and the stars to divide the day from the night and to mark the seasons of the year. And all these things that God had made He saw were good, and they were the work of the fourth day. Then God bade

the sea to bring forth fish and made the birds of the air and told
them to be fruitful and to multiply. And whales came out of the
sea and all other kinds of fish. Eagles took flight, and the birds who
migrate together according to the season of the year were born. And
songbirds sang in joy on all the trees. And that was the work of the
fifth day.

(Lines 450-547) "On the sixth day of Creation and the last, God
called upon the Earth to bring forth the animals that would dwell
upon the Earth itself. And four-footed animals, amphibious beasts,
insects, all came forth in their kind. The new world in all its
beauty and all its richness awaited the master-work: a creature who
would walk upright, able to govern the Earth and to adore God.
Thus, the Father said to the Son: 'Let Us make Man in Our Image,
and let him rule over the fish and the fowl and the creatures of
the Earth.' And that's how He made you, Adam," says Raphael,
"from the dust of the earth, breathing life into your nostrils. He
made you male, then made Eve, your consort, female, and told you
to be fruitful and to multiply and to hold dominion over all the
earth. He placed you in this Garden and gave you but one command: Taste not of the fruit of the Tree of the Knowledge of
Good and Evil.

(Lines 548-601) "And when God looked upon His work, He
found it good in every way. He returned to Heaven while the Earth,
the angels, and the planets all sang His praise, calling upon the
Celestial City to open its gates and receive the great Creator, Who
would go often to visit the new and beautiful world He had made.
Then on the seventh day God and the Son rested, and the Heavenly
Host sang in exaltation of the wonderful works of God:

(Lines 602-640) " 'You were great, O Lord, on the day that You
forced the rebellious angels into Hell. But You are greater now, for
it is greater to create than to punish or to destroy. Who can stand
against You, O Lord? The evil Satan sought to do, You have con-
verted into good. Not only did You defeat Him, but You have con-
founded his plans to limit Your empire. You have made a new and
beautiful world. You have brought good out of his evil. Thrice
happy are the men whom You have made in Your Image to dwell
in this new world, to rule it, and to worship You. All they need
to do is to know their own happiness, and to persevere in doing
right.' So sang the angels," Raphael concludes, "and thus the first
Sabbath was kept. And I have now fulfilled your request, Adam,
and told you how and why your world was created."

COMMENT: Milton's account of Creation amplifies the first two chapters of Genesis and occasionally echoes other parts of the Bible, particularly the Psalms. Milton gives to his version an amplitude and a richness that suggest to the reader a vision of the whole cosmos. He is careful, also, to tailor the account to its dramatic audience, Adam. Note how Raphael reminds Adam that Adam already knows some of the story. For instance, Adam had heard the glorious hymn, the shouts of joy, that accompanied the Son on His return to Heaven.

The events in Book VII represent the first time God brings good out of evil. To defeat Satan would have been only a negative victory. God would have been only the poorer at Satan's defeat. But He uses Satan's rebellion as a reason to make a new world, a world which wrests more territory from the grasp of Chaos and diffuses into new realms the goodness of God. There will have to be a comparable achievement after Adam's fall, or Satan will have won the second round of his battle with God.

PARADISE LOST—BOOK VIII

(Lines 1-65) Adam has been enthralled by Raphael's account of creation. Like one who has been newly awakened, he thanks his guest. There is one thing more he would like to know, though. He asks Raphael why so many heavenly bodies larger than the Earth move so swiftly only to give light to the Earth, a planet, that seems to be stationary. Nature in other matters is so frugal that Adam cannot understand such seeming wastefulness. When Eve realizes that Adam is embarking upon such a difficult subject, she quietly departs to look after her flowers. She is capable of understanding such matters, but it will be much pleasanter, she thinks, to hear the answers from Adam than from the angel. Raphael answers Adam:

RAPHAEL'S ASTRONOMY:
(Lines 66-178) "I do not blame you for asking questions about the stars, for Heaven is the Book of God set before you. But it doesn't matter whether it is the Earth that moves or the heavenly bodies. God, for His own reasons, has chosen to conceal some knowledge, perhaps so that He may laugh at the silly theories your

offspring will advance. You, at the moment, are leading the way. Perhaps the heavenly bodies are larger and brighter than the Earth. That doesn't mean that they are better. The Earth may contain more solid good than the sun. The sun's rays make the Earth fruitful, but the sun is barren itself. Those luminaries in the sky exist, though, not for the Earth but for Man. They help you to know how small you are compared to the rest of the universe and to the God Who made that universe. The huge distances, the speed with which the planets move, are means to keep you humble, too. God has made the universe as He has so that when you speculate about these matters about which you don't really need to know, you will never be sure whether or not you are right. What if the Earth does move and the sun stands still? What if the sun gives light to the moon as it does to the Earth, and the moon, too, is inhabited? Whatever the answers to these questions may be, don't worry about them. God arranges these matters wisely. All you need to do is to serve Him and to enjoy Eve and the Paradise He has given you. 'Be lowly wise.' Think about those things that really concern you, and be grateful for the knowledge of Heaven you have already gained."

(Lines 179-248) "Thank you for solving my doubts," says Adam, "and for teaching me not to let my fancy rove into regions it does me no good to inquire about. It is much better that I fix my attention on matters close to me. You've told me all about what happened before I was created. Perhaps, now, you'd like to hear my story. Day is not yet done, and you can see how I devise means to keep you with me longer. When I talk with you, I feel I am in Heaven. Your discourse is sweeter to me than the sweetest fruits that I have ever eaten. One can eat only so much without feeling filled. But the more I listen to you, the more I want to hear." Raphael replies that he would like to hear "the ways of God with men." He was absent guarding Hell when Adam was created; hence he doesn't know about those events, and he would enjoy hearing about them from Adam.

ADAM'S STORY:
(Lines 249-356) Says Adam, "It is hard for me to speak of the beginning of human life, for how can I know how I began? I awoke on a flowery bed and jumped upright, as instinct told me to do. I looked at all the beautiful things about me with joy, and then I looked at myself. Sometimes I walked, and sometimes I ran with vigorous ease. I didn't know, though, who I was or where I had come from. When I tried to speak, I could, and I knew the names of all the things I looked upon. I asked them if they knew Who had made me. I wanted to know so that I could adore Him. Nothing

answered. I sat down thoughtfully and fell asleep. A dream stood at my head and told me to arise, for He wanted to take me to the garden of bliss that had been prepared for me. He took me by the hand and led me here. When I awoke, I would have wandered further, but then I saw Him and fell at His feet in adoration. He raised me and told me He had made me and had made all the things I saw. I was to be Lord of all about me, but I was not to eat of thé Tree of Knowledge, or I should know death. His stern prohibition still rings in my ear.

"But He went on more pleasantly, telling me that He gave me not just the Garden as my dominion and the dominion of my race, but the whole Earth and everything upon it. Therefore, He was going to bring all those things that lived upon it before me so that I could name them. The animals and birds came before me, two by two, and bowed. I named them and understood their natures. But nowhere did I see the one thing I still wanted. I turned to my Heavenly Vision and said:

(Lines 357-397) " 'I know not by what name to call You, for how can I name what is so much above me. Nor do I know how to adore You Who have been so good to man. But I see no one who can enjoy all these good things with me, and there is no joy in solitude.' 'But the Earth is full of living things,' He replied. 'Rule them and converse with them, for you understand their speech.' The words seemed to be an order, but I begged leave to speak again and said, 'I don't want to offend You, but You have made me Lord of all these creatures. They are not my equals, and there can be no companionship between those who are not equal. I want someone who can share my rational delights. Each of the animals has its proper mate and can pair with nothing else. How, then, can I join with a beast?'

(Lines 398-451) "The Almighty did not seem to be angry when He said, 'It seems you are very careful of the company you keep. And you want no pleasure if you have to take that pleasure alone. Do you think I am unhappy? Yet thefe is no one near to Me in nature at all. I can talk only to those whom I have created, and they are much further beneath Me than the beasts are beneath you.'

'You are perfect in Yourself, Supreme of Things, and are in no way incomplete. Man is incomplete. He needs an equal to comfort him and make up for his deficiencies. You have no need to propagate Your kind, for You are infinite and absolute in Yourself. Man, because he is finite, needs to beget others like himself. That can be done only through mutual love. You can raise those You have made to be fit for Your conversation, but I cannot make the beasts who go prone upon the Earth stand erect, nor can I make them fit to be my companions.' When I had finished, He said, 'I asked you these things, Adam, to try you. I know that none of the beasts is a fit companion for you, and I know that it is not good for you to be alone. I pretended otherwise to see how well you understand yourself. Fear not. The next thing I bring you will be the fit companion, the other self, for which you ask.'

THE CREATION OF EVE:
(Lines 452-499) "He ended His speech, or else I heard no more. The effort I had made to reach the sublimity that conversation with Him required overcame me, and I fell asleep. But my fancy remained awake, and I saw Him open up my side and take a rib, together with the blood and flesh that clung to it. He healed my wound. Then He took the rib and fashioned from it a creature like me but of another sex. She was so beautiful that all the things I had thought beautiful before seemed hardly fair at all. She disappeared, and when I awoke, I wanted only to find her. For without her nothing in the world could please me. Then I saw her, led by her Maker, though He remained unseen. She was as I had dreamed, possessed of every loveliness. I cried out in my joy, 'O generous Creator, this is the fairest of the gifts You have given me. She is flesh of my flesh, bone of my bone, and I shall name her Woman. A man shall leave father and mother to join her, as his wife, and they shall be one in flesh and heart and soul.'

(Lines 500-559) "She heard me, but since she knew her worth, she knew she had the right to be wooed before she granted herself to me. At last she did, and I led her to the bridal bower, as all nature rejoiced in our union. I must tell you that all the other things I enjoy leave my reason always in command. But with her I am weak, made passionate by her beauty. Perhaps Nature made me less than perfect, perhaps took more than enough of my vital spirits from me when she was made from my rib. Or perhaps she was simply made to be too beautiful. I know that she is inferior to me in mind. Even her outward appearance is less truly the Image of God than mine is, since her softness shows less dominion over the other creatures than my strength. But when I see her, she seems to be so complete, so perfect in her loveliness and in all she does and says that my wisdom when I am near her seems to be folly. Reason and authority wait upon her as though she had been created first and made only to be served."

(Lines 560-594) Raphael says sternly, "Don't blame Nature. You have been given all that you need if only you will use your powers. Do not attribute too much to a creature you know to be less perfect than yourself. Love her well, but do not subject yourself to her. Value both her and yourself properly, and she will esteem you the more. And if you are so much moved by sex, realize that it is a faculty you share with the animals. Love your wife reasonably, not passionately. After all, it is because you were made not to sink in carnal pleasure but rather to rise to God by means of love that none of the beasts was a fit mate for you."

(Lines 595-653) Adam, somewhat embarrassed, answers, "It is neither her fairness nor the joy I share with her in the act of procreation that makes me love her so. It is the thousand graceful things she does, the lovely way she has of yielding to me. It seems to show that we truly are one in body and in soul. In other words, I am still choosing reasonably in loving her so deeply. Since you tell me that love is good and is a means for attaining God, will you tell me, too, if the angels can make love?"

Raphael blushes, as he says, "Just let me say that we are happy and that without love there is no happiness. Whatever you enjoy, we enjoy, too, in our higher way since we are purer beings. I can say no more now, for the sun is setting. Be strong, live happy, and love! But remember to love God first and to obey the command that He has given you. Don't let passion sway you, but stand firm in the path that your reason knows is right, and all the Blest shall rejoice in your perseverance."

Adam thanks him, bids him good night, and hopes that he will come often to see them. They part, Raphael on his way to Heaven and Adam to his bower.

COMMENT: Book VIII permits the reader to understand with some clarity Milton's attitude toward knowledge. Adam is encouraged to learn. Raphael, after all, has been sent by God to teach Adam. There is, nonetheless, a limitation imposed upon Adam's quest for knowledge, a limitation other than the one that the commandment not to eat of the fruit of the Tree of the Knowledge of Good and Evil represents. When Adam asks about the heavenly bodies and their relationship to the earth, Raphael's answer is one that would satisfy almost no citizen of the space age. Adam is told that he doesn't need to understand the workings of the heavenly bodies. They are made for him, as is everything else in his world, but their main function, as far as he is concerned, is to keep him humble. He cannot know anything about them with certainty. Therefore, they act as a reminder to him to concentrate on what he can know and to remember how small his wisdom is next to the wisdom of his Creator.

Milton lived at a time when astronomy provided a good example of the uncertainty of human knowledge. The theory that Adam advances when he questions Raphael is the Ptolemaic theory, a theory which naturally appeals to men because it bears out the evidence of their sense impressions. This theory, which held that the earth was the center of the universe and that the sun and the stars revolved around the earth, was being challenged in the seventeenth century by the Copernican theory. Raphael, in his answer to Adam's question, suggests this newer theory: that the sun is the center of the cosmos and that the earth circles the sun.

Milton's position in regard to knowledge is what is usually called "humanist." Man is at his wisest when he concentrates on knowing those things which teach him how to live well and which he can know with some certainty. He is to forgo speculation not only about astronomy but about many philosophic or theological topics as well. In Book II, Milton mentions the devils' futile discussions of such matters as

Providence, Foreknowledge, Will, and Fate—
Fixed fate, free will, foreknowledge absolute—(ll. 559-560)

Such discussions, he says, may be fun, but no one is ever going to come to any useful conclusions by indulging in them. Milton has God state a position on these subjects in Book III, a position that is in accordance with traditional teaching. Obviously, the poet considers the position clear and feels that it is unnecessary to speculate about the question any more.

Adam's Intuition: Not only would men of the twentieth century with their faith in science, then, see Milton's attitude toward knowledge as limited. Men of the Middle Ages, who were convinced of the value of philosophic knowledge, would, too. Nonetheless, the limits are wide. Adam's account of his own awakening to life gives ample evidence that knowledge is one of his gifts. He knows intuitively how to speak. He knows the natures of each of the animals and of all the other created things he sees in his own kingdom.

More important, he knows enough of his own nature to see his relationship to the rest of the world. He recognizes that none of the beasts is a fit mate for him because he is of a higher nature than they. He recognizes, also, that since he is not complete in himself as God is, he needs the society of his equals. Awareness of man's social nature was extremely important to the humanist because man's social needs govern so much of his conduct.

Adam has, also, an intuitive awareness of the fact that he cannot have created himself and that, since he didn't, he owes thanksgiving and adoration to whoever did. Contrast Adam's attitude at his awakening with Satan's boast of self-creation at the end of Book V. Note, also, that Adam *knows* he is far below God, so far below Him that he cannot grasp God's nature. Thus, though Adam can name the animals, he can give no name to God, for the act of naming implies equality to or superiority over the thing named. Adam can name the animals and the plants, as a biologist could name them today, for he can understand what they are. Adam's wisdom in recognizing his inability to give a name to his Creator contrasts, too, with Satan's attempt to prove that he is equal to God.

Raphael's Revelations: Finally, Ralphael teaches Adam many things he could not otherwise know. The revelation about the battle of the angels, and the creation of the world (see Books VI and VII) is given to Adam for his moral benefit. Adam accepts Raphael's teaching eagerly and tries to profit from it. He accepts, also, Raphael's rebuke when Adam asks about what is none of his business—the stars, etc.

Thus, the unfallen Adam represents Milton's ideal of human knowledge. Adam grasps easily many things we find hard to learn. Most biology students, for instance, would find Adam's knowledge of the animals and their natures enviable indeed. Furthermore, he understands himself. He sees his relationship to God so well that he knows he is obliged to obey Him. He learns readily. And his knowledge is obviously his most desirable characteristic. Note God's pleasure in testing him, His joy in Adam's cleverness and in the courage the certainty of his knowledge gives him. God in this section of Book VII is very like any proud parent beaming over his son's good report card.

A Third Trinity: Just as the Son is begotten of the Father and Sin springs from the head of Satan, so Eve is made from Adam's rib. She does not spring from Adam's side full-grown, but is rather shaped by God. But the material God uses comes from Adam. Eve is of Adam's substance just as the Son is of the Father's substance. And the relationship between Adam and Eve is like the relationship between the Father and the Son. It is a relationship of love, and the love is to be creative. From the love of Adam and Eve the new race of mankind is to spring, and that is the race which will complete God's defeat of Satan by permitting the Messiah to be born as Jesus Christ. Note, also, that this relationship between Adam and Eve, the love they share, is what Satan most envies and would most like to destroy, according to his comments in Book IV. If he can make Adam and Eve hate each other, God's plan to defeat Satan will be ended, for there will be no new race to replace the fallen angels, nor will there be a Redeemer for mankind. Thus, the important battlefield between the Holy Trinity and the Satanic Trinity is not really the battlefield of Heaven, described in Book VI. It is Adam and Eve. If what is between them is love, they will bring forth life and be part of the kingdom of the Holy Trinity. If they hate one another, they are going to be sterile, to die without issue, and be part of the kingdom of Hell.

Adam's Uxoriousness: Adam thinks, quite rightly, that the very best thing God has given him is Eve. When he recounts their first meeting, he is much kinder to her than she is to herself. In her own account of her creation in Book IV, she blames herself for the vanity which made her temporarily prefer her own image to Adam. Adam sees the other side of this vanity. He sees her hesitancy as a desire to be courted. Adam says that Eve knew her own worth and, knowing it, knew that she should not give herself lightly. It is her woman's way of letting her lover know that the gift of herself, the only gift she has to give, is a gift of high value. The opinions of both Adam and Eve are right. She needs to value herself, but not to value herself above Adam. If she did, it would mean that she had chosen the sterility of self-worship rather than the fruitfulness of marriage. Danger comes only when her self-respect slips into vanity. Thus far, the dangerous vanity has only been foreshadowed. Eve has not given way to it, yet.

Book VIII foreshadows Adam's fall, too, for it shows the reader

Adam's weakness. Adam's sin, according to Milton, is "uxoriousness," the excessive love of one's spouse. That Milton does
not condemn love between husband and wife is obvious not
only in Book VIII but throughout *Paradise Lost,* especially in
Book IV. What Milton sees as wrong is a love based upon
passion. Adam says that he loves Eve so much that his reason
temporarily is overcome by his passion for her. Most twentieth-
century readers would not agree with Milton's condemnation
of passion, but almost everyone should be able to see with
Milton that one can love one's spouse too much. For instance,
if the husband of a communist spy loves his wife so much that
he becomes a spy, too, even though he doesn't believe in com-
munism, most of us would think that he loved her too much.
Similarly, the man who goes into debt to buy his wife the
luxuries she demands, or the wife who votes as her husband
tells her to, in spite of her own convictions, are both, surely,
guilty of "uxoriousness." Adam's confession of the extent to
which he loves Eve warns us of the chink that is to appear in
his armor.

Another suggestion of Adam's limitations comes in his attempt
to blame Nature or God for his weakness. As he confesses his
almost excessive love of Eve to Raphael, he suggests to the
angel that Nature made him too weak or Eve too beautiful.
Adam's desire to place the blame for his failings on something
other than himself will be evident later, too.

PARADISE LOST—BOOK IX

BEGINNING OF THE TRAGEDY:
(Lines 1-47) Milton begins Book IX by mourning the fact that
he can no longer tell of pleasant discourse between God and man
or angel and man. He must turn now to tragic events: Adam's
failure to be loyal to God and the judgment God was forced to
make upon him. His task is sad, but his theme is quite as heroic
as that of the *Iliad,* the *Aeneid,* or the *Odyssey.* Urania, whom he
had addressed in Book VII, he refers to here as the nightly visitor
who has given him inspiration ever since he decided to write his
epic not about wars or knightly jousts but about the fall of Adam.
With her help he will complete his task, since the glory of his theme
can supply any lack of genius in himself, as it could not, had he

chosen to write of the comparatively trivial matter other epics are devoted to.

(Lines 48-98) On the eighth night, after Gabriel has forced him out of the Garden of Eden, Satan returns. He has in the intervening time circled the earth. He enters the Garden by sinking into the Tigris River and rising as a mist in a fountain near the Tree of Life. He has decided, after investigating all of Earth's creatures, that the serpent will be the best disguise for him to use because the serpent is considered the most intelligent of the beasts. Before he enters into the serpent, he cries out:

(Lines 99-178) "O Earth, you are like Heaven in beauty. Perhaps you are even better than Heaven, since God made you after He had made Heaven, correcting whatever errors he found in that first creation. All the lights of Heaven shine upon you and bring forth the beautiful things you bear, all of which are summed up in man. If I could be happy at all, how happy I could be enjoying your wonders. But I can't be happy anywhere. Good things do nothing for me but torment me because I have committed myself so completely to evil. I couldn't be happy even in Heaven. I gain ease only in destruction, even though I know that only evil will come to me for doing evil. All I want to do is to make others as evil as I am. I want to destroy Adam or win him to do that which will mean his utter ruin. When he is lost, the world that was made for him will be destroyed, too. And I shall boast before the other devils that I destroyed in one day what it took the Almighty six days to build. Who knows how long it took Him to plan it all? Probably, though, He got the idea only on the night when I freed one-half of Heaven's host from inglorious slavery to Him. To get revenge on me and to fill Heaven again, He decided to make these new creatures out of dust. Maybe He couldn't make angels any more—if He ever created them at all. Or perhaps for spite He decided to advance these paltry creatures into our place. The worst indignity of all is that He has set the angels to protect and serve men when men are so much less glorious than the angels are. I must elude the vigilance of these guards, and so I go about cloaked in mist seeking a serpent in whom to hide. How foul a descent that is for me! I, who fought God for mastery of the universe, am compelled to assume the shape of a brute to accomplish my ends. Anyone who aspires finds that he must sink as low as once he soared too high. Revenge may be sweet at first, but its taste is bitter afterwards. I don't care whether it is bitter or not so long as the revenge I take hurts Adam. He has provoked my envy. I may as well lower myself to the level of the serpent, for as high as I can get, I can't be so high as God.

God made this man of clay to spite my followers and me, and the only way to repay spite is with spite!"

(Lines 179-204) The Devil finds a serpent sleeping in the grass. The serpent, not yet poisonous, is sleeping peacefully. The Fiend enters it and waits for morning. When morning comes, Adam and Eve arise, say their morning prayers, breakfast, and discuss the day's work. Since the foliage is outstripping their efforts to control it, Eve says:

(Lines 205-225) "Until there are more laborers, we can't possibly keep up with our work. I suggest, then, that we work separately. When we're together, we spend too much time talking. Hence, though we begin to work early, we accomplish little, and when evening comes, we can hardly say we've earned our supper."

(Lines 226-269) "Your concern about how we might best do our work," answers Adam, "does you honor. However, God has not intended that our work be difficult. We may stop whenever we need refreshment either of food or of the words or smiles our love suggests we interchange. I could, nonetheless, agree to a short absence from you. But I am concerned lest the foe of whom we were warned should harm you in my absence. He is lurking somewhere waiting for a chance to attack us. He knows he is powerless against us when we are together. Thus he will be waiting to catch one of us alone. Let me continue to protect you. A wife is best at her husband's side when danger is near."

(Lines 270-289) Eve replies sweetly, though she shows he has hurt her feelings. "Adam, I know about our enemy, but I am surprised that you doubt my firmness. You do not fear his violence, since we can neither die nor feel pain. Thus, what you fear is his fraud. And that means you fear that my faith and love can be shaken by his fraud. How can you think such a thing?"

(Lines 290-321) "It isn't that I think you are weak," Adam replies. "I know you won't yield to the Devil, but I want to keep him from attacking us at all, for even if we resist the attack, we are somewhat stained by it. The enemy will hardly dare to tempt us both at once, and if he does, he'll try me first. Don't underestimate him. He must be very clever, or he couldn't have seduced so many of the angels. And you shouldn't scorn my help. I know that I will be stronger if I am with you. Don't you feel the same way? Don't you want me, your best witness, to be near when your virtue is tried?" But Eve still feels somewhat insulted:

(Lines 322-341) "If we need to limit our activities so much out of fear, then we can hardly be said to be free. If we're not strong enough to stand alone, we're pretty weak. If the Devil tempts us, the temptation does us no dishonor. Rather he suffers double dishonor when we stand firm. And what is virtue or love worth, if it needs always to be sustained from the outside? God cannot have made us *that* imperfect, or Eden would not be Eden at all."

ADAM DEFINES FREEDOM:
(Lines 342-384) "God has made us as we should be," Adam replies, "but He has made us free. No danger can attack us from without, but because we are free, we can hurt ourselves by choosing wrongly. Thus, I want to protect you not because I distrust you but because I love you. I can help you and keep you from being tricked in case temptation comes in a form you don't expect. Don't seek temptation. Prove your obedience before you try to prove your constancy. But if you really feel that you will be more secure away from me, because you will be expecting trouble, go. For if you remain against your will, I'll miss you even more than if you go. Rely on your innocence and your virtue. God has done His part. Do yours." Eve answers, "I go, then, with your permission, especially because, as you suggest, if we're together, we won't expect to be tried and will, therefore, be less well prepared. Besides, I doubt that Satan will tempt me first. It will be too shameful for him to be repulsed by the weaker of us two."

(Lines 385-472) Eve goes. Adam asks over and over again that she come back soon. She promises as often to be back by noon for lunch or for a nap. But foolish Eve is never really to return. She will never again eat or rest with the sweetness she has always known. For the Fiend has been looking for Adam and Eve ever since dawn, wishing, though not expecting, to find Eve alone. Suddenly he sees her as she is working with some roses. He draws nearer through the beautiful garden. Eve is so beautiful that she assuages his malice. His evil intentions are temporarily blunted, and he stands "stupidly good," unable to do anything. But his envy soon ends his delight in her loveliness. He is tormented even more than he was before because he realizes there is no way in which he can enjoy her. He makes himself hate her the more and does his best to increase his spite:

SATAN'S SPITE:
(Lines 473-531) "What have I been thinking of? I came here not out of love but out of hate. I seek no pleasure, for my only delight is to destroy pleasure. Let me take advantage of the fact that she is

alone. I fear her husband. In my Hell-weakened condition he could defeat me. But she is fair and made for love. I'll conceal my hate under the cloak of love and, thereby, ruin her." He approaches her in the shape of the serpent, which, before the Fall, walked erect. He approaches her indirectly, trying to attract her attention playfully. At first she ignores him, but finally his steady gaze attracts her attention, and Satan begins his temptation:

(Lines 532-566) "Don't wonder, Mistress, that I gaze at you, and don't become angry because I adore your beauty. Your celestial beauty should be adored in Heaven, for here on Earth there is only one man to appreciate you." Eve, amazed because the serpent can speak, says, "How does it happen that you can speak, since God created the beasts to be mute? Redouble the miracle of your speech by showing me that you are rational and explaining to me how it happens that you can talk. And why have you grown so much more friendly to me than the other animals are?"

(Lines 567-612) "I used to be just like the other beasts," says the Fiend, "unable to speak and unable to think about anything but food and sex. Then one day I saw a particularly beautiful tree in the distance. I drew near to it and saw its tempting fruit. I coiled myself about the trunk, for the fruit of that tree is high up in its branches, and ate my fill. Afterwards, I noticed that I was changing. I knew myself able to reason and to speak. I thought about all the beautiful things in Heaven and on Earth and decided that there is nowhere anything so good or so beautiful as you. Thus, I have come to worship you."

(Lines 613-663) Eve, still more amazed, replies, "You praise me so much too much that I'm beginning to doubt the power of the fruit you speak of. But tell me which tree you mean." The Serpent tells Eve that he will guide her to the tree, and Eve agrees to go. He takes her to the Tree of Knowledge. When she sees it, Eve says, "No matter what good the fruit of that tree has done you, I can't eat it. God's only command to us is not to eat the fruit of that tree." The Tempter asks her if she is forbidden to eat the fruit of all of the trees. "No," says Eve, "we can eat fruit from all the others. But if we eat any of this fruit, we shall die."

(Lines 664-733) The Fiend pulls himself up and looks both very wise and very sympathetic. He says, "Thanks to you, O wisdom-giving plant, I can not only understand nature but can also understand why the highest beings in the universe do what they do. Don't be afraid of these threats, Eve. You will not die. I ate the fruit, and

I have not died. I've attained a higher life because I can now speak and reason. God won't be angry with you for daring to eat the fruit. Rather, He'll praise your courage because you will be seeking a better life in spite of His threats. He wouldn't be just if He didn't praise you, and if He isn't just, He isn't God.

"Why was the fruit forbidden, then, since eating it doesn't lead to death? God wants to keep you ignorant so that you'll go on worshipping Him. He knows that when you eat the fruit, you'll know both good and evil, as the gods do. You'll become a god by eating the fruit, just as I have become a man. In that sense, perhaps, you'll die. You'll put off human life to take on a godly life. And that's a death to be sought.

"What are the gods? They got here first and use that advantage to impose on the rest of us. They say they created all things. I don't know that I believe them. I see the Earth producing good things, but I don't see the gods making anything. How could they have made that tree which contains the knowledge they want to keep from you? If He made the tree, surely it would in no way be able to hurt Him. Or does He forbid you simply out of envy? Eat the fruit, and you'll know all these things and many more."

(Lines 734-779) Eve listens to his specious reasoning. She gazes on the fruit, which is tempting in appearance, too. It is, besides, just noon, and she is hungry. She muses, "Your virtues must indeed be great, O Fruit, even though you are forbidden to men. This serpent praises you, and so does God when He calls you the Tree of the Knowledge of Good and Evil. For, after all, knowledge is a good thing. God is simply forbidding us to be wise. Obviously, such a prohibition is not binding. But what if we do die after we've eaten the fruit? The serpent hasn't died, though. Was this food reserved, then, for the beasts? But the only animal who has eaten it offers it to us without envy, having only our good in mind. What do I fear? In my ignorance I don't know enough to fear anything rationally. The cure for my ignorance and my doubts lies in that fruit. I'll eat it and feed at once my body and my soul."

EVE COMMITS THE ACT:
(Lines 780-833) Eve eats, and the Earth groans because all is lost. The serpent disappears, but Eve is paying no more attention to him anyway. She gorges herself on the fruit, thinking to become a god. When she is almost drunk with the fruit, she says to herself: "O Tree, I'll sing your praises every morning and distribute your fruit to everyone. I shall eat until I mature into wisdom like the

gods, who envy what they cannot give. From now on, I'll trust Experience, for if I hadn't listened to experience, I'd have remained forever ignorant. Perhaps I'm doing this in secret. Heaven is too remote to know what I'm doing, and other cares may have made our great Forbidder and all His spies ignore us. Shall I tell Adam, though? Perhaps I'll keep my secret and, because I know all these things I've learned from the Tree, I'll become his equal. Maybe I'll become even more—his superior—and be even more desirable to him than I already am. But maybe God *has* seen, and I shall die. Then Adam will have another Eve and forget all about me: I couldn't bear that. I want Adam to share all my bliss and all my woe. With him I can endure death. Without him I can't enjoy life."

(Lines 834-895) She bows to the tree as if *it* were a god and goes. Adam, meanwhile, has woven a wreath for her welcome. He goes out to find her and meets her near the tree. She has a bough of its fruit in her hand and says, "I've missed you very much, Adam, and I never want to be separated from you again. But this tree we were told was evil isn't evil at all. The serpent ate some of its fruit and became human. I've eaten some, too, and find myself much wiser than I used to be and on my way to becoming like God. I want you to eat it, too, for bliss isn't bliss unless I can share it with you. Eat, because I don't want to be parted from you, and it is probably too late for me to renounce my new-found deity." Eve speaks gaily, but her flushed cheek betrays her inner disorder. Adam, astonished, drops the wreath he has prepared for her and says:

(Lines 896-959) "How could you have done this, Eve? Some fraud of Satan must have led you to your destruction. And I am destroyed, too, for I cannot live without you. Nature draws me to you. What you suffer, I must suffer, too!" Adam, having decided to eat the fruit, too, is comforted and says calmly to Eve: "It's a bold thing you have done, Eve, but it cannot be undone. But, perhaps, you won't die. The serpent, you say, hasn't died, but has rather attained a higher life. I don't think that God will destroy us whom He has created to be lords of the Earth. Then the Devil, in triumph, could say, 'God destroys whom He most loves—first me, now mankind. Who will be next?' At any rate, I am determined that your fate will be mine. Death to me is life, if you are dead. If I lost you, I would lose myself."

(Lines 960-1016) Eve replies, "How can the tree be other than good when it has led to so noble a proof of your love? You would rather die than be parted from me. If I thought eating the fruit really led to death, I'd suffer alone. But it won't. Judge by my experisence and eat." She embraces him and gives him some of the fruit. He eats, knowing that he is doing wrong but unable to bear the thought of losing Eve. Nature groans even more deeply than it did at Eve's sin, but Adam and Eve keep on eating. The two think they feel themselves growing divine. What they are really feeling is drunkenness and lust. Finally Adam says:

(Lines 1017-1066) "Eve, you are to be congratulated for opening up to us the delights this tree offers. But come, let's make love, since you are more attractive to me now than you have ever been." They lie down on a flowery couch, make love, and when they are exhausted, fall into a heavy, dream-ridden sleep. They wake without feeling rested and find their innocence is gone. Ashamed of their nakedness, they gaze at each other mutely, until Adam finally says:

(Lines 1067-1133) "Eve, it was an evil hour when you listened to the serpent. We do, indeed, know good and evil. We've lost the good and gained the evil. We have lost our innocence and our honor. Our love for each other has been tainted by lust, and we are ashamed. How can I face God or the angels now? I would like to live hidden in the deepest shade. But let us take some broad, smooth leaves and sew them together so that we can cover those parts of us that seem most shameful." They take fig leaves and form them into aprons like the garb of American Indians. Thus, the two try to cover their shame, but they cannot ease their minds. They begin to cry and feel for the first time the passions of anger, hate, suspicion, and discord. In this mood Adam says:

(Lines 1134-1161) "Why didn't you listen to me this morning instead of insisting on going off by yourself to try your faith? We'd still be happy if you had."

Eve replies, "Why blame me and my desire to wander. It could have happened if we'd stayed together, too. You would have trusted the serpent, just as I did. After all, what reason had he to wish me ill? Was I never to be parted from your side? I might as well have remained one of your ribs, if that were the case. Besides, knowing that I am the weaker of us two, why didn't you command me to remain? If you had been firm in your opinion and not let me go, none of this would have happened!"

(Lines 1162-1189) "Is this the way you repay my love?" Adam retorts. "Are you going to blame *me* as the cause of *your* sin when I've given up the possibility of immortal bliss in order to remain with you? I couldn't force you to stay. I warned you, but your confidence led you on. Perhaps, I admired you too much. But I'm sorry for that error now. It is my crime, and you've become my accuser. That's what will always happen to the man who trusts a woman too much."

The two go on bickering, each blaming the other, but neither in any way ever truly condemns himself.

> **COMMENT:** The rapid deterioration of Satan's character is evident in his first speech in Book IX. In his long soliloquy in Book IV, Satan was able to face the truth about himself, to admit that he had done wrong. Such honesty is no longer possible. His commitment to evil has destroyed much too much of his original goodness and intelligence. Note how illogical this long speech is: At first he declares that the earth must be more beautiful than Heaven, for God would not have produced a lesser work for His second creation. Then he says he could not be happy even in Heaven, although Heaven is *more* beautiful than earth. Finally he becomes indignant at the notion that the angels are serving men, when men are made merely of dust, dust from that same earth which a few lines before was in his opinion more beautiful than Heaven.
>
> Satan's lies, at first, were for public consumption only. By now, he is lying to himself. He insists that he "freed" half of Heaven's host, even though he knows only one-third of the angels followed him. More important, his more truthful moments in Book IV showed us that he knew he hadn't really freed them. He has become so envious and spiteful himself that he can see only envy and spite wherever he looks. Thus, God has created men and set angels to guard them out of envy and spite. God, in Satan's eyes, is so spiteful that He can be repaid only with spite.
>
> Satan's deterioration is shown, also, in the scene in Book IX in which he first sees Eve by herself. In Book IV he is so much moved by the beauty and goodness of Adam and Eve that he loves them and wishes he could be good to them. He needs to persuade himself to do evil. Here he can be only "stupidly good." He can make no move nor feel any active emotion at all in relation to goodness. The most that he can do is to stand stupidly still, his evil intentions temporarily halted. Thus, Satan has succeeded almost entirely in destroying the natural goodness that was once his as a creature of God. It remains to be seen whether or not he has destroyed his beauty, too.

Satan makes a significant remark at the end of his long soliloquy at the beginning of Book IX when he comments on the fact that he is about to enter into the serpent. He who once challenged God is about to "embrute" himself, force himself into a brute. He says (Lines 169-170) that "who aspires must down as low as high he soared." The lines recall one of Christ's statements: "He who exalts himself shall be humbled, and he who humbles himself shall be exalted." Satan's words confirm the first part of Christ's dogma. The rest of *Paradise Lost* will bear out the truth of the whole of the statement.

The Temptation:　It has been said that Eve got up on the wrong side of bed on the fateful morning of her temptation, that she began the day in a fallen state. It is true, at least, that the morning sees her first disagreement with Adam. But her suggestion that she and Adam work separately is offered in good faith. She is truly concerned about the progress of their gardening. She grows insistent only when Adam tells her he wants to protect her from the Fiend. Everything would probably have been all right, if he had simply told her he couldn't do without her. Eve shows her inexperience and her naiveté when she says that she wants to prove her virtue by testing it. A wiser person would prefer to stay out of temptation. For instance, it is only the very inexperienced person on a diet who stares into the window of the candy store.

Eve's fall comes about in part through her desire, like Satan's desire, to soar too high and partly because she is inexperienced. As she tells Adam at the end of Book IX, she had no reason to suspect the serpent. She has never encountered fraud. If Satan in disguise in Book III could fool Uriel, the archangel, it is not surprising that he can fool Eve. It is true that she should have been suspicious when the serpent said that his new-found wisdom came from eating the fruit of a particular tree. But children are not usually suspicious, and Eve is very childlike. The fact that she is childlike makes her praise of experience after her fall highly ironic. She knows from experience, she says, that the fruit is good for her. It is making her wise. However, she is so inexperienced that she cannot evaluate her own experience accurately. She is confusing drunkenness with wisdom.

Satan tempts Eve by declaring that he loves her. He has hit upon what is both her strength and her weakness. It is her function to love and to be loved, and she knows that it is. Her knowledge, though, can lead her to vanity, as it does in the

temptation scene. Or it can lead her to the graceful dignity
Adam so much loves. Reread his account of his first meeting
with her in Book VIII. Eve is certainly still very much unfallen
and shrewder than one expects her to be when she replies to
the serpent's exaggerated praise of her. He has just told her
that eating the fruit has made him wise and that in his wisdom
he has decided to worship her as the very best being in the
world. Says Eve:

> "Serpent, thy overpraising leaves in doubt
> The virtue of that fruit, in thee first proved." (Lines 615-616)

But her curiosity and her naiveté lead her to follow the serpent
to the tree.

Satan's Guilefulness: Satan's speech of temptation is a
masterpiece, bewildering as it is persuasive. Eve has no chance
to answer one point before the serpent shifts to another. He
has not died from eating the fruit he says. Besides if God is
just, He cannot punish Eve for seeking a higher life. If He isn't
just, then He isn't God. If He isn't God, then He isn't powerful
enough to cause her to die, and Eve need not fear Him. He has
forbidden men to eat the fruit to keep them in awe. If men ate
the fruit, they would be equal to God and would not fear Him.

It is at this point that Satan begins to talk about gods instead of
God. The shift to the plural suggests to Eve that she can be a
god, since there are many gods. It also obscures temporarily
her awed awareness that there really is only one God. Satan
shifts back to the singular pronoun only when he has persuaded
Eve that the only reason she is forbidden to eat the fruit is God's
envy of man. God, thus, in Satan's speech has been reduced in
power, made to seem one of many jealous beings, and finally
made the most envious of the lot.

Eve, tempted by hunger, curiosity, vanity and the devil, eats.
The after-effects of her eating demonstrate, as does the career
of Satan, that whoever soars too high will sink quite low. For
the first time in her life Eve eats gluttonously. Her intellect
is so confused that God becomes the "great Forbidder" and the
angels He has set to protect her become "His spies." She thinks
about keeping her secret from Adam so that she will have more
power over him. She decides to share the fruit with him,
primarily out of envy: she couldn't bear to think of his being
happy with another Eve when she is dead. But when she meets

Adam, she lies to him. She tells him that if she thought he really would die from eating the fruit, she wouldn't offer it to him. Yet she has just said to herself that she couldn't bear either to live or to die without him. The high point of her silliness comes when she, who has set out to become a god, falls down to adore the *tree* as god. She has lost her awareness that *she* is much higher in nature than a tree.

Adam's Sin: Adam commits his sin without any of the extenuating circumstances that surround Eve's act. He knows he is doing wrong. He is not seduced by the wily Satan. He rationalizes his act, saying that God won't live up to His decree because if He does, Satan will be able to mock Him. But it is perfectly clear to Adam and to the reader that he eats the fruit simply because he does not want to be separated from Eve. Ironically, his eating leads to their first real separation, the first time since their creation when they are not one in spirit.

The immediate after-effects of his eating are in some ways like those which followed Eve's sin: he becomes gluttonous and drunk, for instance. Afterwards Adam and Eve taint the purity of their love with lust. They fall asleep, not sweetly as they always have before, but rather sinking into a sodden stupor marred by unpleasant dreams. They awaken to the "morning after" and to a clear awareness of what they have done. Because they know evil, they also know shame. Their innocent nakedness is no longer possible; hence they make aprons of fig leaves to cover their genitals. Milton points out the fact that they look like American Indians, who, to a 17th century Englishman, were the foremost example of savages. These two, who once entertained an angel at dinner, are now reduced to the state of savagery, only a notch higher than the brutes.

Book IX ends with Adam and Eve no longer loving each other, but hating one another. They bicker. They abuse each other and accuse each other, but neither of them is willing to see himself as wrong. It's true that Adam says his crime is that he trusted his wife too much, but that's a crime that makes her fault much greater than his. Eve's answer to Adam is shrewish and absurdly illogical, one of the few truly funny passages in the poem. (See ll. 1144-1161). The two sound not like the gods they set out to become, but like very silly children.

At the end of Book IX, then, Adam and Eve are well on the way to becoming part of Satan's kingdom. If nothing happens to restore the love between them, all they will be able to produce is sterility. And Adam, Eve, and nothing would be a trinity far more unholy than holy.

PARADISE LOST—BOOK X

PITY IN HEAVEN:
(Lines 1-62) God knows, of course, that Adam and Eve have fallen. The angels whom He has sent to guard the two hurry to Heaven to justify their conduct. The angels in Heaven are saddened by the offense but pity the offenders, too. God says to the assembled angels, "Don't be dismayed by what has happened on Earth. The sincerest care of the guardian angels could not prevent Adam's sin. I told you when the Tempter first escaped Hell that man would fall. Since he has fallen, I pronounce the doom of death. I send my Son as Judge, and because I do, you know that I intend mercy, for the Son has volunteered to redeem mankind."

(Lines 63-84) The Son replies, "Your Will is Mine, Father. I will. judge these two as mercifully as possible. As You know, the worst of their punishment must light on Me since I have promised to be their ransom. I'll go alone. There is no need for others to behold the decree. Satan need not be there for the judgment, for his flight already shows that he is guilty."

(Lines 85-125) The Son arrives in the Garden to judge Adam and Eve as evening falls. The two, hearing His voice, hide themselves. God calls out, asking where Adam is. The two come forth, embarrassed and ashamed. There is no love between them, nor do they love God. Their faces show guilt, despair, anger, obstinacy, hate, and guile. Adam says that he heard the voice of God and, being ashamed of his nakedness, hid. God replies that the two have often heard His voice before without shame. And how do they know they are naked? They must have eaten the forbidden fruit. Adam, much upset, says:

(Lines 125-156) "I stand before my Judge and must either accept all the blame or accuse the partner of my life, whose failings I should not expose to blame. But I have to. I can't bear all the punishment myself, and, besides, You would discover anything I tried to conceal. This Woman, whom You made to be my help and who seemed so fair that I trusted her, gave me the fruit, and I ate it." The Son asks, "Was she then your God? Was she made to be your guide that you obeyed her? Had you known yourself and guided her, her beauty would have made you love her in seemly fashion, not subject yourself to her."

(Lines 157-192)   God turns then to Eve to ask her what she has done. Eve, ashamed, says simply, "The serpent beguiled me, and I ate." God says that the principal punishment will fall on Satan, though Adam and Eve are not to know how the devil will be punished. The Son curses the serpent, condemning it to grovel on its belly rather than to walk upright. And He adds, "I will put enmity between you and the Woman. Her seed will bruise your head, and you shall bruise its heel." The prophecy came true when Christ, the Son of Mary, the second Eve, triumphed over death and Hell. The Son then turns to Eve:

(Lines 193-228)   "You will bear your children in pain and sorrow and will be subject to your husband's will." To Adam he says, "The ground is cursed for your sake. You will toil in the sweat of your brow for the bread you eat, and the Earth will bring forth thorns and thistles as well as food. Thus it shall be until you die and return to the ground from whence you came." He pities their nakedness, then, and clothes them in the skins of wild beasts, just as He will clothe their souls in righteousness. He returns, then, to Heaven.

SIN AND DEATH IN COALITION:
(Lines 229-331)   Meanwhile, before Adam's fall and the judgment upon him, Sin, sitting at the now open gates of Hell, says to Death, "Why are we sitting here idly? Satan must be succeeding, or he would have been forced back to Hell. I feel myself growing stronger. I am drawn to a place beyond Hell where there are others who share my nature. And when I go, you must come with me, for Sin and Death are inseparable. But to make it easy for Satan to return, let's build a highway across Chaos connecting Hell and this new world where Satan now rules." Death agrees, saying that he can smell his new victims. The two use the stuff of Chaos to build a wide highway from the mouth of Hell to this defenseless world, now given over to sin. The highway follows the track that Satan had made in his journey in Book II. Sin and Death have just discovered the way to Paradise when they see Satan. Disguised as one of the lesser angels, he is winging his way across the skies.

(Lines 332-353)   After Satan had seduced Eve, he had assumed a different disguise and had watched events up to the arrival of the Son to judge Adam and Eve. Then the devil fled in terror, knowing that he couldn't escape the consequences of his act no matter what he did, but afraid of what God's wrath would do to him if he remained to face that anger at its height. Sneaking back into the Garden at night, he listened to Adam and Eve complain. He gathered from their discourse that his punishment would not take place until some time in the future. He is on his way now in triumph to Hell when he meets his offspring at the foot of the new bridge. He looks at that structure in pleased surprise, and Sin says:

(Lines 354-382) "O father dear, the bridge is *your* work, for Death and I made it, and we are yours. I knew that you had been successful even before I saw you because there is such a great bond of sympathy between us. Hell could no longer hold Death and me. You have achieved our liberty. You have given us the power to build this bridge. All this World is yours now. Your wisdom has gained it even if our Foil in Heaven built it. He can rule in Heaven, but the Earth is yours. His own judgment has decided that it will be. He can either divide the universe with you or test your strength again in battle, for you are now more dangerous to His throne than ever."

(Lines 383-459) Satan sends his daughter-wife and son-grandson to hold dominion on Earth in his name. They are especially commanded to make sure that men are their slaves. Meanwhile Satan will go down into Hell to tell the other devils of his triumph. The two go on to Earth, and he returns to Hell. He ignores the indignation of Chaos, who very much resents having the bridge built over his territory. Satan enters Pandemonium where the legions keep watch. The principal devils are sitting in council, still awaiting his commands. Satan enters in the shape of one of the lowest of the angles and, invisible, ascends his throne. At last he blazes out in what is left of his glory, much to the amazement of his followers. They rush to congratulate him, but he gestures for silence and begins to speak:

(Lines 460-503) "I've come to lead you out of this deep hole in triumph. Now you can possess a spacious World. I've won it for you through perilous adventures, adventures it would take too long to tell you about. I found Man in Paradise, made happy by our exile. I have won him away from his Creator by fraud. And I did it—with an apple. God in His anger has given up His new world to Sin and Death and, therefore, to us. We'll rule over man just as man was intended to rule over the world. It's true that God has assigned some punishment to me—or rather to the serpent whose shape I took. The Seed of the Woman will bruise my head. But a bruise is a small price to pay for the World. Let us, therefore, rejoice and enter into our bliss."

(Lines 504-584) He awaits their cheers but hears, instead, a universal hiss. He has almost no chance to wonder at this turn of events because he feels himself being changed, against his will, into a monstrous serpent. He tries to speak but can only hiss. He looks about and sees that all the other council members are serpents now, too. He is by far the largest, and he seems still to have his power over the others, for they follow him into the open field. As soon as the other devils see him, they, too, are changed into serpents. In their midst a grove of trees, like the Tree of Knowledge, has sprung up. The serpents gaze at the fruit of these trees, afraid that it exists only to shame them further, but too hungry and thirsty to abstain from it. They roll up the trunks of the trees to get at the fruit. But as they eat it greedily, it turns to dust and ashes in their mouths. Some people say that they must undergo this humiliation a certain number of days each year to teach them not to rejoice too much at the fall of man.

(Lines 585-609) Meanwhile, Sin and Death have arrived in Paradise. "Isn't this better," asks Sin, "than Hell, even though it was earned with toil?" "All places are the same to me," answers Death. "All I'm interested in is what there is around to satisfy my hunger. And there doesn't seem to be too much here." Sin responds, "Start on the fruit, and move on up to Man, whom I shall corrupt, infecting all his thoughts and words and deeds and making him your sweetest victim."

GOD'S WATCHFULNESS:
(Lines 610-719) God, seeing Sin and Death go about their business in Paradise, says, "See how those dogs of Hell set out to destroy the beautiful world I made. They think that I have given up the Earth to them. They don't realize that I called them up. I want them to lick up the filth that man's polluting sin brings into the world. When they're glutted, You, O Son, will hurl them through Chaos, sealing up the doors of Hell forever. Then Heaven and Earth shall be made pure and exist together in sanctity." The Heavenly choir sings His praises and the praises of the Son. God, meanwhile, gives each of the angels a particular charge. They rearrange the universe so that the Earth will suffer summer and winter, strong winds and thunder, instead of enjoying the perpetual spring of Paradise. Discord is introduced among the beasts and brings with it death. The animals fly from man instead of viewing him as their friend and lord. Adam

sees some of these changes in the world around him, but they make him less unhappy than does the troubled sea of passion within him. He says:

(Lines 720-844) "Is this the end of the beautiful world God made for us? I wish it were. I'm suffering, but I deserve to suffer. I heard once with delight the command to increase and multiply. But what can I increase now except curses on my head? Whenever anything goes wrong, my descendants will blame me. I'm paying dearly for the fleeting joys of Paradise. Did I ask to be created? Because I didn't, it seems only fair that I should be reduced again to dust, since that's what I want. O God, Your terms were too hard. Now that I've sinned, isn't it enough that I should be punished with death without having to face endless woes, too?"

"But is this the time to complain?" Adam says to himself. "You should have complained when the terms were offered to you. What if one of your sons should say, when you discipline him, 'I didn't ask to be born'? Yet you would have begotten that son only through an act of nature. God *chose* to make you to serve Him. He rewarded you freely. He has, then, the right to punish you, too."

"I submit," Adam replies to his conscience. "It is right that I should return to the dust from which I was made. I wish it would happen soon. How glad I'd be to die, to rest and be secure. What frightens me is that my soul won't die, but will live forever in a living death. But that wouldn't be fair. It was my soul that sinned, not my body; hence it should be my soul that will die. God may be infinite, but surely His wrath is not so great that He will find it necessary to punish me infinitely. But perhaps death is simply this misery I feel extended perpetually. That would be a fair inheritance to leave my sons!"

"O, if only I could take all the punishment upon myself. Why should my offspring who are innocent suffer because I am corrupt? But, then again, since I am corrupt, all that comes from me will be corrupt, too. No matter how hard I try, I can't blame God. I must admit that all this woe is my doing, not His. I only wish that all the suffering could be mine, then, too.

"But that's foolish," he says to himself. "Could you bear that terrible burden even if you divide it with that wicked woman? Thus, you have nothing to hope for. You'll end up like Satan, like him both in your crime and in your fate."

"O Conscience," Adam at last cries, "what a deep and hopeless abyss you have driven me into!"

ADAM'S ANGER:

(Lines 845-913) Adam lies on the cold ground in the black and ugly night—no longer gentle as it was before the fall—bemoaning his fate. Eve, desolate, tries to speak softly to him, but he says: "Out of my sight, you serpent. You should be as ugly as he is so that no one else would be fooled by your beauty. You thought you were strong enough to stand alone, and I believed you! Oh, why did God make such a mistake as to create a woman? Why didn't He people Earth, as He did Heaven, with masculine beings? Then none of this would have happened." He turns away from Eve, but she, in tears, falls at his feet, and embraces them, saying:

(Lines 914-936) "Please don't forsake me, Adam. I know I have offended, but I was fooled by that wicked serpent. What shall I do if you leave me? You're my only comfort in this hour of greatest distress. We may have only one more hour to live. Let us live it, then, in peace and love. Don't hate me. Hate the serpent who seduced me. We are both miserable, but I am more miserable than you. You've sinned against God. I've sinned against both God and you. Your grief is all my fault. I'll ask that God punish me alone, for I'm the one who merits His anger."

(Lines 937-965) Adam is disarmed by her tears and her humble repentance. No longer angry, he raises her gently to her feet and says, "You still want too much to try out the things you know nothing about. You'll have enough to suffer in your own punishment without taking mine upon yourself, too. If I thought prayers would help, I'd ask God to forgive your weakness and blame only me. But let's stop trying to outdo each other in taking the blame. Let's try to lighten each other's burden through the rest of our lives. For it seems to me that the punishment of death will come quite slowly to increase our pain and the pain of our poor children!"

(Lines 966-1012) "Adam," says Eve, "I know I've no right to offer you advice. But now that I've been accepted into your love again, I must tell you what's in my heart. We can spare our children pain by remaining childless. Then Death will have to be satisfied with just the two of us. But if you find it too hard for us to be together and not to make love, then let us seek death now. Why should we suffer so under the fear of death? We have to die anyway. Let's make our pain as brief as possible, and die now." Adam replies to Eve:

(Lines 1013-1104) "I don't think we can cheat God that easily. If we take our own lives to escape His punishment, we would live in death. There is a better way. Remember the sentence passed upon us? In it God said that your seed would bruise the serpent. He must have meant Satan, who in the shape of a serpent deceived us. It would be fit revenge indeed to crush his head. And we'll lose that revenge if we decide to remain childless or to die immediately. Satan will escape his punishment and ours will be doubled. Such an act would be an act of spite against God. Let us, instead, accept His just yoke without reluctance. Remember how mild He seemed when He judged us. We thought we would die that instant. Instead you were given pain in childbirth, but that pain will be repaid by joy when your children are born. I must earn my bread in sweat. That's much better than idleness would be. And to protect us against the cold, He made us clothes, for which we hadn't even asked. Therefore, if we pray, how much more help He'll give us. He'll teach us how to protect ourselves from all kinds of weather, how to have the comforts that we need until it is time for us to return to the dust, our native home. The best thing we can do is to go to the place where He judged us and fall before Him, humbly confessing our faults and begging for His pardon. I'm sure He will relent. For when He was at His sternest, favor, grace, and mercy shone from His countenance." The two, equally repentant, do as Adam has suggested.

COMMENT: Satan's deterioration reaches its final stage in the scene in Hell in which he is boasting of his achievements to his fellow devils. Instead of being greeted by cheers, he hears only hisses— the universal symbol of contempt. He and his followers have been turned into serpents. In striving to exalt himself, to become equal to God, he has become a snake. In his first soliloquy in Book IX, he himself said that if one attempts to soar too high, he will find that he must also sink low. But Satan still persuades himself that he can assume his disguises and do his evil without being essentially changed. At the end of Book IV, he is surprised when the Cherubim who have discovered him at Eve's ear tell him that his external glory has diminished. It has diminished so much that Satan is no longer recognizable as the Archangel who was once Lucifer, the son of the morning.

Since that moment Satan has consistently chosen evil. In doing so, he has consistently destroyed himself. Since he *chose* to be a snake, God has made him into a snake, but Satan had to make himself into one first. All that remains of his great triumph is the dust and ashes he and his fellows taste as they eat the fruit of the tree by means of which they sought to destroy men. He who exalted himself has indeed been humbled.

The Holy Trinity and the Unholy Trinity: Milton, in Book X, once again stresses the contrast between God and Satan by using the trinitarian symbolism. The Son goes as God's regent to judge Adam and Eve. Sin, with her constant companion, Death, goes as Satan's regent to rule the Earth.

But the Son, though He condemns Adam and Eve to death, does it as mercifully and mildly as possible. In the sentence he imposes upon the two, He also holds out hope of life: Eve's seed will crush the serpent who has brought death into the world. And he shows concern for the practical needs of the human couple when He clothes them in the skins of wild animals. He is helping them to sustain life.

Sin's mission, on the other hand, involves total commitment to death. She urges her hungry offspring to destroy all creation beginning with plants, the lowest form of life. By the time Death has completed the first part of his meal, she will have prepared his dessert. She will corrupt Adam and Eve so completely that they are fit only for Death.

That the dominion of the Unholy Trinity is not so complete as it seems to them is shown in the metamorphosis, or change of form, that Satan undergoes in Hell. It is shown, too, in the fact that Death becomes God's servant. It is necessary, God says, that material things die, now that the world has been corrupted by sin. Death becomes a cleansing agent to clear off the waste and the ugliness that Sin brings in its wake. The point will be made again in Book XI. God, then, converts even Satan's instruments to good. Even Death, Satan's child, has its place in God's providence.

Adam and Eve: But if God is to achieve His complete victory over Satan, He needs the cooperation of men. The Son cannot become Jesus Christ, the Savior of mankind, if there is no human race into which He can be born. And it is Christ who will achieve God's final victory, as Book III explains.

Adam, in the beginning of Book X, shows himself to be, for the moment, Satan's disciple. If events depended wholly upon him, there would be no hope at all. When the Son comes to judge

Adam and Eve, Adam blames Eve first, and then blames God
for having given her to him. In his long soliloquy he sounds
much as Satan did in his first soliloquy in Book IV. There is
even the same manifestation of a "split personality." Adam
talks to himself in the second person, just as Satan did. And
as Satan saw the justice of God in that one moment of truth,
so Adam sees that his punishment is just, too.

The principal difference between the two speeches is that Satan
determines that his only course is evil. Adam doesn't know
what to decide. He is caught in his agony of remorse. He is
unable to pray, for he can see no point in asking anything of
God. (Satan felt that way, too.) Adam's position as the father
of mankind holds only bitterness for him because he can will
his descendants only pain. And all he will get from them is
blame. For that matter, there is some doubt that there will ever
be any descendants for Adam because Adam feels only hatred
and contempt for Eve. He is utterly incapable of feeling any
sort of compassion for her. If everything depended on Adam,
then, the Human Trinity would be Adam, Eve, and Death,
staunch citizens of the kingdom of Hell.

The person who returns the Human Trinity to the dominion of
God is Eve. And she does it in the only way possible—through
love. From the beginning of Book X she appears in a better
light than does Adam. When she is judged, she says simply,
"The Serpent fooled me, and I ate." Though she is not at that
time ready to repent, she shows none of Adam's desire to push
the blame off on to someone else. Furthermore, she is capable
of compassion. When she sees Adam suffer, she can forget her
own pain in sorrow for his. She humbles herself before him
and wins him once more by means of her love.

Milton has been accused of being anti-feminist, but Book X
surely denies the truth of such a judgment. Eve is the key
figure in the reconciliation of Adam and Eve, a reconciliation
that is absolutely necessary if God's plan to defeat Satan is to
be successful. Eve is less intelligent than Adam, but it is her
primary function not to know, but to love. That function she
fulfills admirably. The reader may say that the first move was
up to her, that Adam was right in blaming Eve, for, after all,
she had sinned first. God, in Milton's poem, however, does not
agree with such an interpretation. Reread the Son's speech in
answer to Adam's complaints against Eve (ll. 144-156).

After the reconciliation, Adam again takes his rightful position as leader. Eve's humility and love have restored their natural relationship. Unable to see any way out of their trouble, she suggests suicide. Adam, no longer angry and bitter, can, because of Eve's love, fulfill his function now, too. He recalls the words spoken at their judgment. And he sees hope in the prophecy that Eve's Seed will crush the serpent. He remembers, too, God's kindness to them when they had no reason to expect Him to be kind. With more wisdom than his wife, he sees that their immediate death will accomplish nothing and that their life offers reason for hope.

Book X ends with Adam and Eve humble before each other and humbling themselves before God. When the two of them sought to exalt themselves by becoming gods, they became silly children. Now their humility will bear witness to the truth of the second part of Christ's saying: "He who humbles himself shall be exalted."

PARADISE LOST—BOOK XI

PRAYER AS WORSHIP:
(Lines 1-44) With the aid of divine grace, Adam and Eve pray humbly and repentantly. The Son says to the Father: "See the fruits of the grace You have given to man—these sighs and prayers I bring to You. They are more pleasing than any fruit that the trees of Paradise could have produced under Adam's care before he fell from innocence. Accept his prayers. I'll make up for anything they lack, just as by My death, I'll atone for man's sins. Let men live in reconciliation with You for My sake. I ask to mitigate his doom, not to reverse it, so that during his sad, short life he may live in such a way that he can dwell in Heaven with You for all eternity."

(Lines 45-83) "I grant Your request," says the Father, "but Adam can no longer live in Paradise. That place is intended only for the undefiled. I gave him two gifts when I created him: happiness and immortality. Now that he has lost the first, the second could only make his woe everlasting. Thus, Death has become man's final remedy. If he lives well, it will also be his entry into eternal life. Call together all the blest so that they may know My judgment upon both men and the fallen angels." The Son signals a ministering angel, who blows his horn, summoning all the heavenly spirits to gather about the throne of God. When all are seated, God says:

(Lines 84-140) "Man has decided to become like one of us, knowing both good and evil. He has repented by means of My grace. But just in case he becomes bold enough to try to attain eternal life by eating of the Tree of Life, I must send him out of Paradise. Michael, you are to force Adam out of Paradise. Take warriors from among the Cherubim with you in case Satan is planning some new mischief. Tell Adam that he and his progeny are banished from the Garden forever. Do not frighten them. If they obey the command willingly, tell them what will happen in the future, reminding them of My promise to the Woman. Send them forth in peace, and set Cherubim to guard the eastern entry and the path to the Tree of Life. I don't want some foul spirit to tempt man with its fruit." Michael prepares to depart, accompanied by Cherubim, each of which has four faces. Morning has come again to the Garden. Adam and Eve are comforted by their prayer, though they are no longer so confident as they were before their transgression. Adam says:

(Lines 141-180) "Eve, though it may seem strange that anything we do should influence God, still as I prayed, I was sure I saw God listening. I am sure that I was heard with favor. I remembered His promise to you that your Seed should bruise the serpent. The bitterness of death, then, is past, and I can rightly hail you the mother of mankind." Eve replies, "I don't really deserve that title, for I who was made to help you became your snare. But God's pardon to me is infinite, for I, through whom Death entered the world, am made the source of life. But we must get to work, since it is morning. Though our work is to be toilsome, it can't be very bad if we can still live in this pleasant place. Let us live here in contentment, even though we are no longer perfect."

(Lines 181-225) Fate will not grant Eve's wish, however. Adam notices that the lion is chasing the deer toward the eastern gate and that an eagle is stooping to capture two gaily plumaged birds. There is, as well, an eclipse of the morning sun. He says, "There will be some other change in our state, Eve, or else what do all these omens mean?" By this time, the Heavenly bands have reached the Earth, providing a sight too glorious for Adam's sin-dimmed eyes. Michael, telling his followers to take possession of the Garden, advances to the place in which Adam has taken shelter. Adam sees him and says to Eve:

(Lines 226-285) "Someone very powerful is coming from Heaven to bring us important news. I must meet him with reverence, and you must retire." Michael approaches in the shape of a man, carrying his dread sword and also a spear. Adam bows to him, and Michael says: "Adam, Heaven has heard your prayer. You will not die immediately but will live long enough to atone for your sin by many good deeds and to be completely redeemed from Death's claim. But you may no longer live in Paradise." Michael says no more, for Adam is struck dumb by the news. Eve, who has heard the news from her place of retirement, cries out, "How can I leave Paradise where I had hoped to end my sober days? How can I leave the flowers I have tended or the bridal bower I adorned so sweetly? How can we breathe the grosser air of the world beneath this mountain? To leave this place is worse than death!"

(Lines 286-333) Says Michael, interrupting her, "Do not lament your loss, Eve, for you have no right to Paradise. And you will go with Adam, not alone." Adam, having recovered, says, "You have told us this painful decree as gently as possible, Celestial One. All other places seem to us so desolate that I would bombard Heaven with prayers to be allowed to remain. I know, though, that there is no point in asking God to change His absolute decree. Therefore, I submit. What makes me saddest is that I shall no longer be able to converse with Him face to face or show my sons the places where He appeared to me. Where shall I seek Him in the world below? I fled Him once in anger, but I long now for just a glimpse of His glory, and from a distance I would adore His steps."

MICHAEL'S LESSONS:
(Lines 334-369) Michael says gently, "Don't think that God is only in Paradise. His presence may be felt throughout the Earth, His great gift to you. Paradise might have been your capital, the place to which all your sons would come to venerate you as their great progenitor. By sinning, you have lost that preeminence and must dwell on equal footing with them. But God will follow you and wrap you in His paternal love and care. That you may believe He will, I am going to tell you, at His request, what is going to happen to your offspring in the future. You'll hear much that is good and much that is bad. From the story learn to be patient and to be in all things moderate so that you may live your life successfully. Then you will be unafraid to die when the time comes. Let us go up that hill and leave Eve here asleep while I tell you about the future."

(Lines 370-428) Adam says that he will follow Michael and learn

the lessons the angel has to teach. They ascend the highest hill in
Paradise, from which they can see the whole eastern hemisphere.
It is the same hill to which Satan took Christ when he wanted to
tempt Him to be untrue to His mission. Perhaps, in spirit, Adam
saw the western hemisphere, too. With three drops from the well
of life, the angel clears Adam's eyes of the film that has covered
them because of Adam's sin. Then Michael tells him to look upon
the results of his sin.

(Lines 429-499) Adam sees Cain and Abel make their offerings
to God. Because Abel's is accepted and Cain's is not, Cain murders
the other out of envy. Adam is appalled both at the sight of death
and at the fact that Abel seems to suffer for doing good. Michael
tells him that Abel will be rewarded and Cain punished. He tells him,
also, that Death will come in many ways, but that the entrance to
death will always be more frightening than death itself.

Michael next shows Adam the results of gluttony. Adam sees a
hospital. Its deformed inmates are suffering agonies from all the
maladies that come from intemperance. Adam weeps at the sight,
saying:

(Lines 500-555) "How dreadful that mankind should suffer such
degrading pain! Why are we forced to live if we must die so
fearfully? Surely we should be spared such ugliness and pain if
only because we are made in the image of God!" "Their Maker's
image deserted them," retorts Michael, "when they began to behave
like brutes." Adam agrees that the pain they endure is just but asks
if there are any less painful ways to die. "Yes," replies Michael,
"if you live temperately, you can die peacefully of old age. But in
old age you will no longer be strong or handsome, nor will you
be able to enjoy the good things of life." Adam says that he will
no longer fly from death, but will seek to live his life as well as
possible so that he may be able to accept death whenever it comes.
Michael agrees that, though living well is Adam's business, the
length of Adam's life is up to God.

(Lines 556-637) The next scene prepared for Adam shows the
discovery of music and the discovery of metal, both of which take
place on a spacious plain. At the same time, a group of godly men
who worship God and live soberly descend from the hills onto the
plain where they see some beautiful women coming out of tents
pitched upon the plain. They marry one another. Adam thinks this
scene is much pleasanter than the ones he has been before, but
Michael tells him not to judge the worth of reality by pleasure

alone. He tells Adam that the women and the inventors are the descendants of Cain. They are very clever, but they do not worship God. The Sons of God (who are the descendants of Seth, the third child of Adam and Eve) are the men who came down from the hills. The women they marry are beautiful but empty-headed and vain, and they will soon corrupt their husbands. Adam pities the men and blames the women, but Michael says that the fault really lies in the weakness of the men. They are too effeminate to use their authority properly.

(Lines 638-711) Next, Adam sees gigantic men in scenes of violence and war. A man stands up to argue for peace and justice. But he is saved from the anger of his fellowmen only because he is taken up to Heaven in a cloud. The violence, injustice, and oppression go on unabated. Adam asks who these terrible men are and who the righteous speaker is. Michael tells him the giants are the children of the ill-matched marriages of the previous vision. These giants will be famous, he says, and will be honored for their strength as if they were gods, even though they are really destroyers. The righteous man is Enoch, who will live seven generations after Adam. Because of his justice, he will be exempt from death to show how the good will be rewarded. Adam is to look next at the punishment of the wicked.

ADAM GRIEVES FOR THE WORLD:

(Lines 712-762) Adam sees men living riotously. A just man preaches to them, but they ignore him. He moves to the mountains and builds a huge ship. Two each of all the species of animals enter the ship, as does the just man, his three sons, and each of their wives. God fastens the door of the vessel, and the earth is flooded. Everything is destroyed except the Ark. Adam grieves to see his children destroyed and says to the angel:

(Lines 763-839) "I would be better off not knowing the future. Then I would have to bear only my own pain instead of enduring the suffering of my offspring, too. Man, then, needs to be warned of nothing more, for the few who were saved in the Ark will die, too. Tell me, Celestial One, is this how the race of man will end?"

Michael tells him that the riotous livers are the giants who conquered the earth but who had no true virtue. Weakened by sloth, they will be conquered too, and will live dissolutely on whatever their conquerors give them. They will lose all faith in God when the piety they pretend to have during the time of their danger does them no good. Noah, the one just man, at God's command will build the Ark against the flood. The flood will destroy Paradise, forcing it into a gulf where it will be an island inhabited only by animals of the sea. For no place is sanctified in the eyes of God unless men make it holy by good deeds.

(Lines 840-901) Then Adam sees the waters evaporate and the Ark resting on dry ground on the top of a high mountain. A raven and then a dove are sent out from the Ark. When the dove returns bearing an olive-leaf, Noah and his family come out of the Ark. They kneel in prayerful thanksgiving and see a rainbow. Adam rejoices more at the fact that the just man is saved to beget a new world than he sorrowed to see the evil men destroyed. He asks the meaning of the rainbow. Michael tells him that it is the sign of God's promise not to destroy the Earth again by flood. The world will go on in its daily course until it has been purged by fire and has been merged with Heaven as the home of the just.

COMMENT: God's victory over Satan, His ability to bring good out of evil, is manifested in many ways in Book XI.

The Son says in the first episode in Book XI that the humble and repentant prayers of Adam and Eve are the fruit of God's grace, a fruit more pleasing than any that Paradise before the Fall could bring forth. He means, of course, not only that these prayers are higher in nature than is the physical fruit of the Garden's trees. The prayers are better, too, than any of the acts that the human couple performed in their state of innocence.

Adam and Eve before the Fall are very attractive. But a careful reader who compares their conduct at the end of Book X with their conduct before their encounter with the Serpent cannot but be aware of how childlike they are in the beginning. They are so sure that they can do no wrong. They—especially Adam —are given to making such pompous speeches. It is true that their delight in their beautiful garden, in each other, and in their own ability is charming. But it is charming as the conduct of good children usually is. Look again especially at Adam's account, in Book VIII, of his conversation with God shortly after God has created him. Note again that Milton presents him as a clever child being tested by a proud parent. Similarly, Eve slips away from Adam and the angel at the beginning of Book VII because she would rather hear about astronomy from

Adam than from Raphael. Her coyness is attractive and quite lovable. But it has about it also an air of girlishness, rather than of womanliness.

The couple at the end of Book X has grown up. Eve, when her love for Adam makes her humble herself before him, behaves in the fullness of her womanhood. Adam, when he forgives her, speaks not with the smug pomposity that marks many of his early speeches to her, but with simplicity and directness. As he gropes his way toward comfort and tries to find new reasons for the two of them to live, he shows none of the cleverness that marked his earlier exchange with his Creator. But he shows qualities far more mature and far more valuable: He is steady, serious, able to deal soberly with grave doubts, a feat far more difficult than it is to reason glibly before we have seen cause to doubt.

None of these statements are intended to deny that Adam and Eve before the Fall were good. They were, but in their innocence they were good as children are good. In their fall they became wicked children. In their repentance they truly rise to new heights. They grow up. And in doing so, they make one of Satan's statements come true. In Book II, Satan told his followers (ll. 14-16):

> From this descent
> Celestial Virtues rising will appear
> More glorious and more dread than from no fall.

The statement could not be less true for Satan and his fellows. The only way in which they can see to act is to rebel against God once more. They seek to rise by rising *against* God. It is true for Adam and Eve, for they in humility see their faults. They ask Heaven's help. They rise *with* God not against Him, and thus make it possible not only for good to come out of the evil they have done as good comes out of Satan's evil. The good touches them personally, too, as no good can affect the fallen angels.

The "Happy Fall": Milton's attitude toward Adam and Eve after their fall is in accord with the Christian doctrine of the "happy fall." The happiness comes first of all from the fact that if Adam had not sinned, Christ would never have been born. But Christians felt, too, that the Fall made men able to be better, too. Innocence is all very well as far as it goes. But to be humbly aware that one is a sinner opens up the way to far more beautiful virtues: tolerance, compassion, understanding, charity. Such virtues are almost impossible for the innocent, for in their innocence they have no way of understanding other people's weakness. They need to see themselves as weak before they can feel fellowship and understanding for the weakness of others.

The experience of Adam and Eve parallels, also, universal human experience. All of us move from the brittle innocence of childhood through a discovery of evil to the charity that accepts our own failings and those of our fellow men. That is, we grow up to such charity if we allow ourselves to accept, as Adam and Eve do, the lessons our weakness can teach us. Such acceptance is possible, Milton is saying, because God offers us the grace by which we can understand ourselves and Him. We need only to choose to accept that grace, as Eve chooses to accept it when she begs Adam to forgive her.

The Goodness of Death: Book XI mentions again an idea introduced in Book X. In a fallen world, a world corrupted by sin, death is not an evil but a good. Adam and Eve must leave Paradise, God decrees. Yet the decree is not a harsh one. To permit the two to remain in the Garden to eat of the fruit of the Tree of Life would be not kindness but cruelty. Their life, tainted by sin and sorrow, needs to end. To live immortally in such a state would be intolerable. Death, furthermore, for the good man, is entry into a new kind of life.

Adam echoes God's statement after he has learned from Michael of the ways in which men will die. He comes to know that even the most temperate of lives needs to be ended by death: Men, subject to sin, will grow old, lose their vigor and their energy, and will, if they have lived well, be ready to die. A comparable idea is presented in Book III of *Gulliver's Travels* when Gulliver visits the land of the Struldbrugs, who are born to be immortal. (See, also, the poem "Tithonus" by Tennyson, a poem about a figure in Greek mythology who was given the gift of immortality without having also been given the gift of eternal youth.)

Adam and Women: It is interesting to note that Adam still cherishes some of his grudge against Eve. When he is told of the ill effects of the marriages between the women of the plain and the Sons of God, he says (ll. 632-633):

I see the tenor of Man's woe
Holds on the same, from Woman to begin.

Michael needs to remind him, as God did, that if women succeed in leading men astray, it is because the men do not behave
in a manner that accords with their manliness.

Adam's Vision: The history of the world that Michael shows
Adam covers the material in the *Book of Genesis,* Chapters IV
through IX. Book XI ends with another example of God's bringing good out of evil: the rescue of Noah, the one just man, and
his family in the Ark so that a new race can come upon the
earth with another chance to live righteously. The last image
of Book XI is the rainbow, a traditional symbol of hope. It is
God's covenant with Noah, His promise that He will never
again destroy mankind. Men will live on Earth until the end of
the world unites Heaven and Earth.

PARADISE LOST—BOOK XII

(Lines 1-78)   Michael pauses in case Adam has any questions and
then says that in order not to weary Adam, he will tell Adam the
rest of the story instead of showing it to him in visions. "This second
race of men will at first live in peace. Then Nimrod, who will not
be content to be among equals, will claim dominion over others.
He will become a hunter of men. He will try to build a tower that
will reach to Heaven in order to be famous forever. But God will
make each of the builders speak a different tongue. Since they will
be unable to communicate with one another, their project, called
the Tower of Confusion or Babel, will fail." Adam is quite dis-
gusted to hear that one of his sons will claim dominion over the
men who are his equals and who should be free.

(Lines 79-269)   Michael explains that one of the results of Adam's
sin will be the loss of true liberty. For since men will not always obey
reason, they can't be said to be truly free. Because of men's un-
reasonableness, God justly permits them to suffer the loss of outward
liberty, too. But the tyrant is not to be excused, even though God
does permit tyranny. The new race, after Nimrod, will go from
bad to worse, as did the first. God, in disgust, will withdraw His
presence from them. He will choose a nation sprung from Abra-

ham, who will serve the true God, even though he is the son of an idol-worshipper. God will promise Abraham that from his seed will come a nation in whom all men will be blessed. The seed is that Deliverer who will crush the head of the serpent. The land of Canaan will be given to Abraham and his nation. Abraham will have a son and a grandson. The grandson and his twelve sons will leave Canaan for Egypt, where they will live at first as guests. Later Egypt's king will become suspicious of them and make them slaves. They will be led out of their slavery by Moses and Aaron after the Egyptian tyrant has been subdued by terrible miracles wrought by the power of God. Moses will lead his people to Canaan through the desert in which they will form their government. God on Mount Sinai will give Moses laws governing the life of His people and their manner of worshipping Him. Moses will be an intercessor between God and the children of Abraham. Thus, he will foreshadow the Intercessor for all mankind that his nation will produce. In His pleasure at this holy people, God will set up His Tabernacle among them. The Tabernacle will travel with these people on their way to Canaan. After many battles, Israel, as this nation shall be called, for that is the name of Abraham's grandson, shall win the promised land.

(Lines 270-371) Adam says that he is relieved to hear about Abraham and his descendants, but he wonders why it will be necessary for God to make so many laws, especially since Israel is to be a just nation. Michael replies that, like the rest of Adam's descendants, the Israelites will be sinners. Having the Law will teach them that though the Law can discover sin, it cannot atone for sin. The Israelites will realize, then, that a Redeemer is necessary, and their faith in His coming will justify them before God. Because the Law is only the precursor of the true Redeemer, Moses, the lawgiver, will not be allowed to lead his people into Canaan. They will be led by Joshua, whom the Gentiles call Jesus. And that is the name the Messiah will bear. Meanwhile, the Israelites will dwell in Canaan, at first under Judges and then under Kings. The second king will be David, the psalmist. God will promise that his house will reign for all eternity, because the promised Messiah will be born from it. But before the Messiah comes, the Israelites will live under many kings, more of whom are bad than are good. They, themselves, will fall into idolatry, and God will permit them to be taken captive to Babylon. They will be brought back to their own land after seventy years. The people will live in moderation at first, but later dissension will arise, and priests will steal the sceptre, no longer paying heed to David's sons. Thus, the Messiah will be born barred of His right to the throne. At His birth a star will proclaim

His arrival and guide three sages from the East to His crib. An angel will announce His birth to shepherds. A virgin shall be His mother but His father will be God Himself, and He shall reign over Heaven and Earth.

ADAM'S UNDERSTANDING:

(Lines 372-465) Michael pauses because Adam is weeping tears of joy. Adam says that now he understands why the Deliverer has been called the Seed of Woman. He will be born of a virgin, but, nonetheless, He will be Adam's son. Adam asks, then, in what kind of duel the Messiah will bruise Satan. Michael tells him that there will be no duel between Satan and the Messiah. The Messiah will defeat Satan by destroying Satan's works in mankind. And He will be able to only through obedience, just as Adam could have defeated Satan through obedience. "He will undergo your punishment," says Michael, "by living as a man and dying a shameful death. In His death all your pain will die. He will rise again on the third day, and thus shall sin and death and Satan be defeated. After His death He will appear to His disciples, charging them to teach all nations, not just the Seed of Abraham, what they have learned from Him. He will ascend into Heaven and rule at God's right hand, judging both the living and the dead until the Earth has been purified into a new Paradise."

(Lines 466-484) Adam in joy says, "I don't know whether to repent of my sin or whether to rejoice in that God will bring so much good out of the evil I have done. But tell me, what will happen to the few who are faithful to Him after He has ascended into Heaven? Will they not be treated as badly as He was?"

(Lines 485-551) "Indeed they will," says Michael, "but God will send them a Comforter, the Holy Ghost, to guide them in truth and to arm them against Satan. They will be able to withstand whatever men do to them. The Holy Ghost will enable them to speak in many languages and to the people of many nations to lead them to belief in the Messiah. They will write an account of their doctrine before they die. But they will be succeeded by Wolves who will use the sacred truths to their own advantage, giving themselves titles to which they have no right. They will force men to obey laws instead of allowing them to live by Faith and Grace. Many will persevere in the truth, and they will be persecuted. The world will always be good to the evil and do evil to the good. Finally, the Messiah, your Savior, will destroy Satan and this perverted world. From its ashes He will build a new Heaven and a new Earth in which the just will live forever in peace and joy."

(Lines 552-573) Adam says, "You've covered all of time very quickly, and eternity I know I cannot comprehend. I am well instructed and will not seek again to know what I have no right to know. I know now that it is best to love, obey and trust in God. I know that suffering for the Truth is the best kind of bravery and that, to the faithful, death is the gateway to life. I know all this through the example of Him Who will be my Redeemer."

(Lines 574-609) Michael says that Adam has achieved the highest wisdom. If he will add good deeds and the virtues of faith, patience, temperance and love to his knowledge, he will not mind leaving Paradise. For he will possess a much better Paradise in his own heart. "Let us descend from this mountain," Michael concludes, "for the time has come for us to leave this Garden. The angels I have told to camp here are waving their swords as a signal. Awaken Eve. I've sent her dreams to calm her and to make her patient and submissive to God's will. Tell her what I've told you, especially about the promised Seed so that you can live together in a common faith." They descend, and Adam finds that Eve is already awake. She says:

(Lines 610-649) "God has told me in a dream where you've been and why, and I have awakened comforted. Let's go, for if I'm with you, I am in Paradise no matter what place we're in. And I know, too, that my Promised Seed will restore all that my sin has lost."

Adam does not answer, though he is well pleased, for Michael is waiting to escort them out of the Garden. The Cherubim glide into their defensive positions, and the flaming sword of God precedes them. Michael takes Adam and Eve in either hand and hurries them out of the eastern gate and down the cliff. He disappears. Adam and Eve look back at Paradise and naturally weep a little because they are leaving the only home they've ever known. But their tears are soon dried. The whole world is before them, and Providence is their guide. Slowly, hand in hand, they walk alone through Eden.

COMMENT: Book XII continues the history of the world begun in Book XI, a history which reaches its climax with the birth of Christ. It also continues the themes of that book. Thus, Adam voices the doctrine of the Happy Fall, discussed in the comment to Book XI, in lines 469-478. Now that he knows of the coming of Christ, he says, he doesn't know whether to weep for his sin or to rejoice because of it. The life of Christ, he realizes, will make possible an even higher life for men than Adam's innocence could have achieved.

What this higher life will be is made clear, too. Milton knows
that the coming of Christ did not eliminate sin. What it did do
was to teach those men who are willing to learn how to live in
a world so many of whose citizens are committed to evil. Christ
promised no Utopia. He promised, rather, peace on Earth to
men of good will. He promised to make it possible for such
men to live by means of faith and grace in peace with God and
with themselves. Michael explains to Adam what that peace
will be. If Adam has faith, virtue, and charity, he need not fear
to leave Paradise. For he will possess "A paradise within (him)
happier far" (ll. 587).

Michael's words recall one of Satan's earliest boasts (Book I,
ll. 224-225):

> The mind is its own place, and in itself
> Can make a Heaven of Hell, a Hell of Heaven

The words have proved ironically true of Satan over and over
again as he has been forced to admit in Book IV and again in
Book IX that he cannot leave Hell. He carries Hell within himself no matter where he goes. He can be no more truly happy
on Earth or in Heaven than he is in Hell, for he carries his
torment with him.

For Adam and Eve the words prove true in another way. They,
too, have learned that their peace and happiness depend upon
themselves, not upon their surroundings. The Garden of Eden
is only a setting. They were as unhappy there right after their
fall as they had been happy before. They can have happiness
wherever they go, a surer happiness than Paradise provided, if
they preserve their obedience to God and their love for one
another. As Eve says (ll. 615-18):

> with thee to go
> Is to stay here; without thee here to stay
> Is to go hence unwilling. . . .

Eve's Final Realization: Eve has realized that she can do
without the flowers in Paradise she has been accustomed to tending and that she can build another bridal bower like the one
she was at first so reluctant to leave. What she needs is Adam
and the peaceful awareness that God will right the wrong she
has done. She can go forth calmly to become the Mother of

Mankind, knowing that the title is glorious even though she does not fully deserve it.

Thus, we are prepared for the poignant ending when Adam and Eve, hand in hand, wander away from Paradise to build their new paradise together. The peace and love they feel toward each other and toward God mean that the Human Trinity will be not Adam, Eve, and Death, but Adam, Eve, and living children —and ultimately the Child who is the Christ.

CRITICAL COMMENTARY

Milton attracted little critical attention in his own time, but in the twenty-five years following his death leading critics of the period such as Dryden and Roscommen rated him very highly as a heroic poet. In the early eighteenth century, Addison's essays on *Paradise Lost,* which were frequently reprinted, introduced Milton to a wider public.

ADDISON (1712): Addison examined *Paradise Lost* "by the rules of epic poetry," according to the criteria set up by Aristotle in his *Poetics.* He concluded that Milton's epic consisted of one entire action, comprising a beginning, middle, and end, "contrived in hell, executed upon earth, and punished by heaven." The whole work had "indisputable and unquestioned magnificence." As for the characters, he thought Adam and Eve in their innocence both finer and more original than anything in Homer or Virgil. After the fall, the pair were marked by guilt and infirmity, but even so were representative of us all and therefore interesting. With regard to sentiment, Addison thought Milton excelled all poets but Homer, especially in his first, second, and sixth books. He only objected to the passage where the devils rally the angels on "the success of their newly invented artillery." This passage he found full of poor puns. With regard to language, Addison observed that an epic should avoid the forms and phrases of ordinary speech, and admired Milton's metaphors, his Latinisms (such as inversion), and his use of antique and also newly-coined words, all of which he found proper to blank verse. Next Addison treated Milton's defects. He was troubled because the outcome of the plot was unhappy and because the hero, whom he identifies as the Messiah, was "by no means a match for his enemies." He found the episodes of Sin and Death and that which dealt with the Limbo of Vanity improbable. There were too many digressions, too frequent allusion to "heathen fables," too much ostentatious learning, too many foreign idioms, too many jingles, and too many technical terms.

Eighteenth-century Milton criticism, according to Thorp (*Milton Criticism*), focused on Milton's religious teaching, which was regarded as orthodox. Milton's heresies were not noticed. He was praised for his "sublimity," in accordance with the teaching of Longinus, who was much admired in this period. But Richard Bentley edited *Paradise Lost* in 1732, altering many passages to suit his own taste. In his edition, for example, the last two lines of the poem became

> Then hand in hand with social steps their way
> Through Eden took, with Heav'nly comfort cheer'd.

DR. JOHNSON (1779):   Dr. Johnson, too, although he thought Milton sublime, had some criticisms to offer which were to prove influential. He was rather critical of Milton's early poems. He found them neat, elegant, and original, but "too often distinguished by repulsive harshness." "The rhymes and epithets seem to be laboriously sought, and violently applied." *L'Allegro* and *Il Penseroso* he admired and wrote of with sympathy, but his comments on *Lycidas* seem peculiarly perverse. He thought it insincere ("where there is leisure for fiction there is little grief"), and found the language harsh, "the rhymes uncertain, and the numbers unpleasing. . . . Its form is that of a pastoral, easy, vulgar, and therefore disgusting." With the fictions of the poem "are mingled the most awful and sacred truths." *Comus* he found "truly poetical," embellished with allusions, images and epithets, but deficient as drama, "inelegantly splendid and tediously instructive."

Paradise Lost he rated highest in design and second in performance "among the productions of the human mind." Because of the nature of its subject matter, he thought it "universally and perpetually interesting." The design has organic unity. Milton is great in his power to astonish; he has "the power of displaying the vast, illuminating the splendid, enforcing the awful, darkening the gloomy, and aggravating the dreadful." "Sublimity is the general and prevailing quality in this poem." The sentiments [ideas], based as they are on scripture, breathe "sanctity of thought." The epic had some deficiencies, however. Johnson felt a lack of human interest. The story of Adam and Eve is almost too familiar. There are incongruities in Milton's descriptions of the spirits, when he tried to invest them with living bodies. The allegory of Sin and Death is inconsistent and faulty. Adam is awkwardly made to speak as if he knew other men, while he and Eve are still supposed to be the sole creations. The Paradise of Fools is ludicrous.

Paradise Regained Dr. Johnson found elegant and instructive, but lacking in action. As to *Samson Agonistes,* he felt that Milton had been mistaken to model it on Greek dramas "with their encumbrance of a chorus," rather than on French and English drama. In general, he thought Milton not equipped to excel in drama, being deficient in real knowledge of men.

ROMANTIC PERIOD (1800-1825):   In spite of Johnson's strictures (Thorp notes), Milton continued to be admired and imitated in the eighteenth century, though often uncritically. Critics of the romantic period showed a new interest in his technical achievements. Hazlitt, for instance ("On Shakespeare and Milton," 1818), shows how Milton could convey "the grandeur of the naked figure," in effect like a sculpture. He instances the picture of Beelzebub:

> With Atlantean shoulders fit to bear
> The weight of mightiest monarchies

and the imaginitive picture of Satan compared with the huge Leviathan. Hazlitt also praises Milton's marvellous ear for music in his verse. "The sound of his lines is moulded into the expression of the sentiment, almost of the very image. They rise or fall, pause or hurry rapidly on, with exquisite art. . . ." Also of significance in this period, is the interest in Satan and Satanism. "The nineteenth-century interest, beginning with Blake and Shelley, tended more toward crystallizing in Satan's character the impact of the poem or even toward commending the moral and ethical codes that he represented. The force of the Satanists' beliefs (as they developed during the later nineteenth century) is really an attack (sometimes unconscious) on the underlying ideas of *Paradise Lost*—an attack that obliquely condemns the poem for enshrining false and pernicious theological, moral, and ethical notions" (Thorp, p. 9).

DE DOCTRINA CHRISTIANA AND AFTER (1825-1860): The publication of Milton's long-forgotten doctrinal statement, *De Doctrina Christiana,* in 1825 should have been a milestone in the history of attitudes to the poet, because it showed quite clearly that Milton held some opinions which were heretical. The fact that it did not create much stir showed that *Paradise Lost* was no longer chiefly thought of as a bulwark of orthodoxy. Emerson, for example, remarked, "We have lost all interest in Milton as the disputant of a sect." He saw him rather as a great and inspiring man, "dear to mankind, because in him . . . humanity rights itself; the old eternal goodness finds a home in his breast and for once shows itself beautiful." He thought of Milton as an example of magnanimity and of Christian holiness rather than as a dogmatist. Milton was still admired for his artistry. Landor, for example, though he admitted to being averse to "everything relating to theology," loved "the harmony of *Paradise Lost*," and said that after reading it he could take up no other poetry with satisfaction. "In our English heroic verse, such as Milton has composed it, there is a much greater variety of feet, of movement, of musical notes and bars, than in the Greek heroic; and the final sounds are incomparably more diversified." Tennyson praised Milton as the "mighty-mouthed inventor of harmonies . . ./ God gifted organ-voice of England." Some other critics, such as Hunt and Ruskin, noted the artificial nature of Milton's style, but regarded it as uniquely his own and rightly so.

MID- AND LATE-VICTORIAN (1860-1915):   In this period, says Thorp (p. 12), "Milton the Man and Milton the Thinker were dismissed for the sake of Milton the Artist." David Masson's six-volume life of Milton pictured the poet as a disagreeable, haughty, bigoted Puritan. Controversy followed as to whether Milton only became unpleasantly Puritan after about 1640 (before that being influenced by the Renaissance as well), or whether he was merely by nature strict and harsh, quite apart from Puritan influences. The ideas in his poetry were not much discussed and Milton was not taken seriously as a thinker. He was admired almost solely as an artist. Arnold spoke of "the sure and flawless perfection of his rhythm and diction," and says he was "a great artist in the great style." He goes on, revealing his opinion of Milton's subject matter, "Whatever may be said as to the subject of his poem, as to the conditions under which he received his subject and treated it, that praise at any rate, is assured to him." The stress was on Milton's ability to write sonorous verse. The ideas it expressed were neglected.

MODERN CRITICS, 1915-PRESENT: In modern times Milton has been reconsidered as a man, as a thinker, and as an artist. Denis Saurat's *Milton, Man and Thinker* (1919), reclaimed for Milton some status as a thinker. He deals with Milton's "system" (his word) at length, taking into consideration his ontology, cosmology, psychology, ethics, religion and politics. He shows that Milton was a systematic thinker in all these areas. Though many of Saurat's ideas about Milton have since required correction, he was a pioneer in claiming that Milton was a thinker in any serious sense. He also had a fresh view of the character of Milton, whom he called a "man of action and of passion." From his youth Milton was marked by a lively and deep sensitivity and by "a sort of moral intractableness, which led Milton to sacrifice every practical or sentimental consideration to a high ideal of purity and truth, in private or public life." This latter trait is usually identified as Milton's Puritanism and has impressed most readers and biographers, who have often done less than justice to Milton's more human qualities. Saurat shows how Milton's correspondence with his friend Charles Diodati reflects, for example, his love for the theatre and his "intense susceptibility to feminine charm." The Italian sonnets also reflect Milton's susceptibility to woman, as well as his "marvellous sympathy with nature" and its fecundity. United with Milton's sensitivity is his passion of self-mastery, especially in the form of chastity, which he believed would give him greater powers as a poet. Milton perhaps took himself too seriously and trusted too completely in his reason, but this is because his sense of mission is so great. "Literary ambition and pride of intellect are the dominant factors in Milton's youth."

In the Cromwellian period Milton became a man of action, writing pamphlets for the Parliamentary side in their struggle against the Bishops. For this struggle for liberty Milton was, thinks Saurat, consciously sacrificing himself and the work for which his genius was destined. However, becoming a man of action in the political sphere made him in the end a better epic poet. "The problem of evil had appeared to him in all the bitterness and despair of personal failure and of vain suffering and vain sacrifice." *Paradise Lost* became a "song of hope and comfort to the vanquished."

Saurat thinks Milton's marriage to Mary Powell was a severe shock. He believes that Milton was "carried away solely by physical passion" and that Mary "refused herself to him" and shortly after left him. The divorce pamphlets show Milton's horror of separation in spirit from one's mate, of being chained brutishly to one whom one did not love. Milton's highest ideal, that of love as a harmony between body and spirit, was at once shattered and soiled." The notion that the Fall occurs generally and painfully through a woman began to take shape.

Saurat claims that Milton suffered another shock when he found that the Presbyterians were as willing as the Bishops "to force our consciences that Christ set free." In *Areopagitica* Milton appealed to Parliament to abolish censorship. His attitude was egotistic and personal: "He finds out how narrow-minded the Presbyterians are —when they won't allow him to settle his private affairs as he likes; and the necessity of the freedom of the press—when they want to prevent him from publishing his tracts." Milton was further disappointed with Cromwell's religious policy. He wanted the disestablishment of the church and the suppression of paid clergy and continued to write in favor of this even after Cromwell died. His last pamphlet before the return of Charles II dealt with *The Ready and Easy Way to establish a free Commonwealth, and the Excellence thereof, compared with the inconveniences and dangers of readmitting Kingship in this Nation.* The title demonstrates Milton's naiveté and daring. In 1660 the King returned and the "good old cause" was lost. How was the triumph of the enemy to be explained? "The failure of all the terrestrial hopes of the Puritans made something more of *Paradise Lost*. Disaster gave the poem that vital and impassioned interest which makes of it more than a work of art, the ultimate question of man interrogating destiny." Milton finds in man both the causes of his failure and the capacity to shape his own destiny. If man by obedience and self-discipline would amend himself, he would amend his fortunes. In *Paradise Lost*, "Milton, once·again, comes to the rescue of Man in his struggle against the Fates."

MILTON'S RELATION TO THE RENAISSANCE: Meanwhile, other critics were trying to relate Milton as a thinker to the Renaissance in general, not merely to Puritanism. Edwin Greenlaw, for example, tried to show how *Paradise Lost* was influenced by Spenser. James Holly Hanford in "Milton and the Return to Humanism" (1919), drawing on studies which re-examined Milton's debt to Spenser and other Elizabethans, showed that "Milton's true kinship is not with Bunyan or Baxter, nor yet altogether with Cromwell . . . but with those men of the olden day, whose spiritual aspirations were united with the human passion for truth and beauty and who trusted the imagination as an important medium for the attainment of their ideals." Spenser, the Fletchers, and Herbert would have understood *Paradise Lost*, whereas Bunyan would probably have not. Milton's basic beliefs—in God, in sin, in retribution, in reward in heaven—were not peculiar to Puritanism, but were held by all humanists of the Renaissance period. Milton showed his humanism in the way he handled the scriptural materials. He believed they could be interpreted by individual judgment and treated them freely, boldly, and imaginatively. *Paradise Lost becomes* "the epic of man's moral struggle, the record of his first defeat and the promise of his ultimate victory." Milton's belief in freedom within a framework of discipline, his "Platonic subordination of the lower faculties of man to the higher," his zeal for knowledge, and his respect for truth all put him on the side of the humanists. The pioneer work of Greenlaw and Hanford was continued by such scholars as Tillyard, Woodhouse, and Bush. "These scholars pointed out the fusion of Protestant and Renaissance elements in Milton's thought and maintained that, although Milton was perhaps not a profound and original philosopher, at least he was a thinker, and a thinker not circumscribed by theology" (Thorp, p. 17). *The Renaissance and English Humanism* by Douglas Bush (1939) may be taken as representative of this group. Claiming that "the classical humanism of the Renaissance was fundamentally medieval and fundamentally Christian," Bush shows that Milton, with his "lofty faith in God and human reason," is "the last voice of an essentially medieval tradition," in which the poet stands with such a twelfth-century humanist as John of Salisbury. "Partly as a young Baconian, partly as a young Platonist," Milton attacked the "sterile Aristotelianism" of Cambridge. He had all the idealism and optimism of the earlier Renaissance thinkers. Stirred by nature in spring and by the beauty of young girls he sees, Milton still clings to his Christian virtue. "Thus the young Renaissance artist and the young Puritan live in happy harmony together." Milton also took seriously his function as "poet-priest," and his desire to live "As ever in my great Task-Master's eye," echoes Pindar as well as the Bible. *Areopagitica*, Milton's defence of liberty and of the power of truth, is in form a classical oration, but historically "grew out of a Puritan controversy over the rights of religious minorities." The letter on education is only "the last of the long series of humanistic treatises which had begun nearly three hundred years before, and it has all the main features of the tradition," its goal being the training of the ablest young aristocrats to be "useful and cultivated citizens." Milton's "emphases on religion and virtue in the discipline of the moral judgment and the will, is no special mark of Puritan zeal, for that had been the chief end of Christian humanism." Milton is allied to the humanists in his passionate belief in free will. "No humanist who had learned from the ancients the dignity of human reason could accept predestination and the depravity of man." Milton interprets the distinction between the regenerate and the unregenerate in humanistic (i.e., rational and ethical) terms, rather than in Puritan terms. He is concerned in his major works with the theme of man confronted with temptation, and these temptations are seen as much in classical terms as Christian—i.e., the struggle is between unreason and reason as much as between the love of God and the flesh. This is clear also in *Paradise Regained*. Christ triumphs, not so much on the cross, as in the struggle against the temptations. The denunciation of Greek culture (by Christ) in this same poem only shows that when Milton is forced to choose "between the classical light of nature and the Hebrew light of revelation," he had to choose the latter. A similar ambiguity may be seen in Milton's attitude to science. A Baconian in his early years, he yet made Adam learn "the necessity of temperance in pursuit of secular and scientific knowledge." He had come to fear that speculation might undermine more fundamental values. "For all his rationality and radicalism, in his conceptions of God and man Milton stands with Erasmus and Petrarch and John of Salisbury. . . ."

ATTACKS ON MILTON: While Tillyard, Bush, and Woodhouse were pursuing their scholarly enquiries, attacks on Milton as an artist came from Ezra Pound, Middleton Murry, T. S. Eliot, and F. R. Leavis. It will suffice to summarize the last two.

Eliot blamed Milton for the destruction of the unified sensibility of the early seventeenth century from which he thought English poetry never recovered. In an early essay on Milton (1936), he found him "as a man, antipathetic." "Either from the the the moralist's point of view, or from the theologian's point of view, or from that of the political philosopher, or judging by the ordinary standards of like-ableness in human beings, Milton is unsatisfactory." Though a great artist, he has been a bad influence, not only in the eighteenth century, but later. "Milton's poetry could only be an influence for the worse, upon any poet whatever." At that date Eliot felt it was an influence "against which we still have to struggle."

The trouble with Milton, Eliot thought, was that he was powerfully aural, but lacked a strong visual imagination. His senses were "withered early by book learning," and his blindness increased a natural tendency to depend on his ear. His language is artificial and conventional. His imagery—for example the plowman, the milkmaid, and the shepherd in *L'Allegro*—is general, not particularized. Their effect is solely on the ear. Words in conjunction do not light one another up, as they do in Shakespeare. In fact Shakespeare's language in effect "split up into two components one of which was exploited by Milton and the other by Dryden." Of the two, Dryden's language, being more conversational, was the healthier of the two. Milton's style, on the other hand, is rhetorical so that "a dislocation takes place, through the hypertrophy of the auditory imagination at the expense of the visual and tactile." *Paradise Lost* has to be read twice, once for the sound, once for the sense; whereas in Shakespeare or Dante both can be appreciated simultaneously.

As for subject matter, Eliot then saw only a "repellent" theology and a myth which would have been better "left in the book of Genesis, upon which Milton has not improved."

Eliot concluded that "Milton may have done damage to the English language from which it has not wholly recovered."

F. R. Leavis in *Revaluation* (1936), praises Eliot for Milton's "dislodgment," accomplished, he notes, "with remarkably little fuss." He himself regards Milton's grand style, in *Paradise Lost,* as somewhat hollow, "commonly the pattern, the stylized gesture and movement, has no particular expressive work to do, but functions by rote, of its own momentum, in the manner of a ritual." He thinks the style gets in the way of concrete realization and of sensuous particularity. Moreover, Milton's habituation to Latin in order and constructions cut him off from the essential expressiveness of the English language. Milton's Latinized obscurities testify to "a callousness to the intrinsic nature of English. Milton forfeits all possibility of subtle or delicate life in his verse." Even the consummate art of *Lycidas is* "incantatory, remote from speech." Leavis even questions Milton's often praised architechtonics—"a good deal of *Paradise Lost* strikes one as being almost as mechanical as bricklaying." "The belief that 'architectural' qualities like Milton's represent a higher kind of unity goes with the kind of intellectual bent that produced Humanism—that takes satisfaction in inertly orthodox generalities, and is impressed by invocations of Order from minds that have no glimmer of intelligence about contemporary literature and could not safely risk even elementary particular appreciation."

Biographies from this period which should be read are E. M. W. Tillyard's *Milton* (1930) and J. Holly Hanford's *John Milton: Englishman* (1949). Both contain critical appraisals of the poems. Of specialized interest is Donald L. Clark's *Milton at St. Paul's School* (1948). Clark is currently working on a book on Milton's university years.

INTRODUCTION TO MILTON'S STYLE: A valuable introduction to Milton's epic is C. S. Lewis's *Preface to Paradise Lost* (1942). Lewis distinguishes primary epics such as the *Iliad and Beowulf* from secondary epics such as Virgil's *Aeneid,* and shows that after Virgil the "merely heoic" will not suffice: "The expressly religious subject for any future epic has been dictated by Virgil." Milton was to choose such a religious subject. In a chapter on "The Style of the Secondary Epic," Lewis points out that the grand or elevated style is produced by the use of unfamiliar words and archaisms, the use of proper names "splendid, remote, terrible, voluptuous or celebrated," and frequent allusion to sense experience (such as light and darkness, storms, flowers, love, etc.), all carried out "with an air of magnanimous austerity. Hence comes the feeling of sensual excitement *without* surrender or relaxation, the extremely tonic, yet also extremely rich, quality of our experience while we read." Milton is in fact "'drawing out the Paradisal Stop in us.'" Lewis defends the right of a rhetorical poet to manipulate his readers and to call forth stock responses in them. He shows that when Milton speaks of himself in *Paradise Lost*, it is not as an individual, but in his character as the Blind Bard, which is appropriate to the poem. Lewis also has valuable chapters on Milton and St. Augustine, Satan, Milton's angels, sexuality before the Fall, and the Fall itself. All are stimulating and written in Lewis's own personal and attractive style.

In *Paradise Lost in Our Time* (1945), Douglas Bush takes issue with the attacks on Milton, particularly that of T. S. Eliot's which he examines in full, showing that his comments betray "a lack of perception and understanding." Unfortunately, he points out, "Mr. Eliot has done more than any other individual to turn a generation away from Milton," mainly because "the poetic world was not big enough to contain both Milton and Mr. Eliot, and Milton had to go." On his part Bush claims: "I do think that the house of poetry, non-dramatic poetry, has many mansions, and that Milton still occupies the royal suite." In his second chapter, "Religious and Ethical Principles," Bush set out to show that Milton's world-view still has significance for us. Milton sees man as a religious and moral being in a religious and moral universe. The goal of man's education, as stated in the *Tractate* on that subject, "is to repair the ruins of our first parents, by regaining to know God aright and out of that knowledge to love him, to imitate him, to be like him, as we may the nearest by possessing our souls of true virtue, which being united to the heavenly grace of faith, makes up the highest perfection." Milton's curriculum included science, but was mainly based on the ancient classics and the Bible. In *Areopagitica* he claimed the right to free discussion, though safeguarding basic religion and morality and admitting some censorship of books after they were published. Milton believed that after Christ's coming, the law of the gospel replaced the law of Moses, and man became, "through divine grace and his own insight and effort," a "self-directing son of God." This gave man liberty, but not license; he was still responsible to God for all he did. Allied with this teaching on wise, responsible liberty was Milton's principle of "right reason." This reason is implanted in all men by God. It distinguishes man from beasts and enables him, within limits, to understand the purposes of a God who "is perfect reason as well as perfect justice, goodness, and love." Reason, including the highest pagan wisdom (such as Plato's), is God-given; but for the Christian it must be supplemented by "Christian revelation and love." Bush stresses this theory because, as he points out, the anti-Miltonists such as Middleton Murry have apparently not heard of it.

WHAT GOD MEANT TO MILTON: Milton's God represents not only power and love, but the rule of reason in the universe, in society, and in the soul of man. These three realms are united in the great chain of being, the whole of creation making up a divine harmony. While Christ is "the incarnation of divine love and the atonement the great manifestation of that love," Milton also stressed Him as "the great exemplar' of right reason. As God represents right reason in the universe (the macrocosm), the soul represents it in man (the microcosm).

In justifying God's ways to man, Milton stressed two points, the love and grace which make regeneration possible, and man's freedom to exercise right reason in making moral choices. He elaborated the Adam and Eve story to show that Eve falls through weakness of reason, Adam through weakness of will. Both violate the principle of reason or order in the universe and consequently become "an unnatural chaos of contending passions." The root of their sin, of all men's sin, is pride. Religious humility must be learned. Adam learns that through humility he may "gain a new Eden within his own soul." Bush points out that Milton's own personal faith was tried and tested. He was full of confidence and hope in the early days of Cromwell's regime, optimistically expecting the regeneration of the English people. He underwent a long series of disillusions, "in bishops, kings, parliament, people, army, even Cromwell." After the Restoration all his work seemed to have gone for nothing, he was blind, his hopes were blasted. His faith was tested and he emerged with certainty that "in His will is our peace," the theme of his three major poems. He saw pride and the will to power "overthrowing the divine and natural order in the world and in the soul," and sent out "a serious call to a devout and holy life." Bush thinks the poem can still shake our pride and lead us to repentance. "We need the shock of encountering a poet to whom good and evil are distinct realities, a poet who has a much-tried but invincible belief in a divine order and in man's divine heritage and responsibility, who sees in human life an eternal contest between irreligious pride and religious humility."

In 1947, T. S. Eliot gave a lecture on Milton before the British Academy in which he qualified some of the earlier opinions associated with his name. He still admitted to "an antipathy towards Milton the man," but questioned whether Middleton Murry was

right in supposing Milton was a bad influence on Keats. Milton
has merely made great epic "impossible for succeeding generations,"
as Shakespeare made "great poetic drama impossible." Keats might
have written a great epic, but Shakespeare's influence on *King
Stephen* was probably even worse than Milton's on *Hyperion*. Eliot
qualified some of his statements about Milton's influence in his
1936 essay. The notion that "Milton's poetry can *only* be an influence for the worse" must be qualified, for the responsibility rests
with those who are influenced. The idea that the destruction of
unified sensibility should be blamed on Dryden and Milton Eliot
also withdrew. "If such a dissociation did take place, I suspect that
causes are too complex and too profound to justify our accounting
for the change in terms of literary criticism." Eliot retains the
opinion that Milton's style is eccentric—"there is always the maxi-
mal, never the minimal, alteration of daily language," but thinks
this a feature of his "peculiar greatness," as is his sense of structure.
As to whether Milton's influence is beneficent or otherwise, Eliot
is still doubtful. He observes at one point "Even a small poet can
learn something from the study of Dante, or from the study of
Chaucer. We must perhaps wait for a great poet, before we find
one who can profit from the study of Milton." However, he concludes his essay with the statement ". . . it now seems to me that
poets are sufficiently removed from Milton, and sufficiently liberated
from his reputation, to approach the study of his work without
danger, and with profit to their poetry and to the English language."

E. M. W. Tillyard supplemented his *Milton* (1930) with *The Miltonic Setting: Past and Present* (1947) and with *Studies in Milton*
(1951). In the latter book, the essay on "Adam and Eve in Paradise" is of particular interest. Tillyard shows that the activities
pursued by the pair are those appropriate to a honeymoon. Their
life as described is not yet perfect and developed. Had they re-
sisted Satan's temptations, it would have changed and become richer.
Their love was as yet self-sufficient, "unrival'd love/ In blissful
solitude." Their gardening activities were merely a prelude to their
love-making. Their "Gard'ning labour then suffic'd/ To recommend
cool Zephyr, and made ease/ More Easie, wholesome thirst and
appetite/ More grateful." "They were on holiday," claims Tillyard,
"they had no job." It is absurd to say that their life was dull.
Their gardening tasks foreshadow their future toil as their loving
courtship foreshadows their future generation. Eve's "fruitful womb"
will fill the universe with her descendants. Similarly, Paradise will
be fruitful; it is "The seminary of all creation." Both Eve's fruitfulness and the garden's will be fulfilled in the hereafter.

In "The Christ of *Paradise Regained* and the Renaissance Heroic Tradition." Tillyard agrees with Merritt Hughes that the theme of the renunciation of glory in the world "was a matter both of traditional interest and very much alive in Milton's own day . . . Milton's Christ as an exemplary hero is of the central Renaissance type; and as the perfect shape of virtue, fulfils the requirements of Protestant neo-platonism." But he thinks that this theme also reveals Milton's private thoughts at the time. Milton had already shown himself concerned in the poems on the nativity, the circumcision, and the passion, with the union of activity and resignation in Christ and with the balance between the two. "It is one of his master-themes, felt through every fibre of his nature." In Milton's life the balance between action and contemplation was upset while he was writing the pamphlets against the bishops. Tillyard thinks Hughes is wrong in seeing "a heroic, otherwordly Christ" in *Paradise Regained*. Rather he finds the emphasis in the poem "unduly on the passive virtues." He compares Adam's last speech in *Paradise Lost* with Christ's refutation of the world in *Paradise Regained*. "Christ speaks superbly but somehow he protests too much." The poem does not express the active tendency of Milton's mind as do the major poems.

Tillyard's *The Metaphysicals and Milton* (1956) is also stimulating. Recalling that when enthusiasm for the Metaphysical poets was revived, Donne was often compared favorably with Milton, it attempts to dislodge the accepted idol. Warning us that "it is perilous to talk of schools of poets at all in the first half of the seventeenth century," Tillyard proceeds to contrast the two poets. He first examines their sonnets to their dead wives, Donne's "Since she whom I lov'd hath paid her last debt" and Milton's "Methought I saw my late espoused saint," noting three contrasts. First, Donne's sonnet is self-centered, focusing on his own grief and stupefaction, whereas Milton "has his eye on his deceased wife and not on himself." He honors her and treats her as a real woman, comparing her to Alcestis and to "one of the ancient archetypes of religious practice in the old Hebrew world." Secondly, he observes that Donne's logical structure is contradictory. He makes a statement—that his mind is set on heavenly things—reverses it by saying that he still thirsts for his own wife, and then reminds himself that his wife's love "has been superseded by the infinitely inclusive love of God." Milton, on the other hand, does not reverse himself as Donne does. He proceeds steadily from the idea of Katharine Woodcock, pale as Alcestis, pale in the ceremony of purification "from child-bed taint," to Katharine glorified, as already in heaven. Her countenance still shone with "love, sweetness, goodness," but as she bent to embrace him, the poet woke to his sense of blindness and loss. "Milton does not rush to his end; he embellishes the way to it; but he has it steadily in mind." The poem is conventional, in the best sense of the word, whereas Donne's is studied. Donne is interested in the complexity of his own often conflicting thoughts, whereas Milton is always working toward his resolution—e.g., in the apotheosis of *Lycidas,* even when he digresses from it in speculating whether Lycidas visits "The bottom of the monstrous world" or sleeps by St. Michael's mount in Cornwall. Donne likes to suspend conclusions, whereas Milton is always "questing" for a resolution.

G. A. Wilkes in *The Thesis of "Paradise Lost"* (1962), is another defender of Milton. He points out that "The central issue . . . is to be decided substantially by an appeal to what happens in the poem. The hindrances to his design—the unsympathetic presentation of God, the seductive appeal of Satan, the nobility of Adam in his wrongful choice—may be freely recognized. But they must still be seen in perspective, assessed in their relation to the total scheme of the poem." The epic does not deal merely with man's fall, but also with his redemption. It covers the revolt of the angels, the war in heaven, the creation, the fall, and the history of man to the birth of Christ. ". . . *Paradise Lost* is a treatment of the operation of Providence, traced through the celestial cycle from the revolt of the angels to the Last Judgment, and its purpose is to justify the workings of Providence to mankind." The epic has to be read as a complete study of the intentions and actions of God. As such it satisfies.

In *Milton's Epic Voice* (1963), Anne Davidson Ferry studies the epic from the point of view of the language used by the narrator. The poet who speaks is at once the blind bard, an inspired seer, and fallen man who is dismayed that Eden has been lost. He knows, however, that the Eden within may be regained if man uses his will and makes the right choices. Redemption is available. The narrator's style gives unity to *Paradise Lost.* Metaphor, allegory, and parody all play their part. The narrator is important in sustaining the "Great Argument" of the poem.

ESSAY QUESTIONS AND ANSWERS
FOR REVIEW

1. The character of Satan is a study in the destructive power of evil. Show how Satan destroys himself through his commitment to evil by tracing his deterioration from the haggard though still glorious Archangel of Book I to the monstrous serpent of Book X.

ANSWER: Satan, in Books I and II, is still unmistakably an Archangel, even though the careful reader becomes aware that he already shows some of the destructive effects of his commitment to evil. We admire his brilliant rhetoric, and most of us sympathize with his character as a proud rebel who will not submit even though he knows he has been defeated. We sympathize, also, with the sorrow he feels when he looks on the pain of his defeated comrades. He is, however, a liar, and the fact that he is one is shown not only throughout the rest of *Paradise Lost* but even in Books I and II. For instance, at the beginning of Book II he tells his fellow devils that they have an advantage over the forces of God because there can be no envy in Hell. But at the end of the conference of devils in that same book, he is very careful to take steps that will keep the other devils from enviously stealing his glory.

It is at the end of Book II that Satan shows himself to be truly, by nature, a creature of God, not a creature of evil. When he encounters Sin and Death at the gates of Hell, he is at first repelled by them. They are hideously ugly, and Satan, created to be the highest angel in Heaven, cannot fail to recognize their ugliness. He is forced to recognize them as his own when Sin explains who she is. He cannot deny that Sin and Death are his, that he begot them. But, in another sense, he does violence to his nature by accepting them. When he chooses to recognize them instead of choosing to repudiate them forever and return to the world of goodness for which he had been created, he is choosing to do evil. And that is a choice that does violence to his own nature.

Satan assumes his first disguise at the end of Book III. He approaches Uriel, the guardian of the sun, in the shape of a lesser angel. Uriel is at first fooled by Satan's disguise, but Satan betrays himself at the beginning of Book IV when Uriel observes his tortured countenance as Satan meditates upon his state. It is interesting to note that Satan is unaware that he has changed outwardly. He is still convinced that he can do evil without his nature's being changed. He must acknowledge that his circumstances are changed, that Hell is very different from Heaven, but he fails to realize that when he makes Sin and Death his allies, he is bound to be changed, to become like them in some way.

The soliloquy at the beginning of Book IV is immensely important, not only because the external evidence of Satan's torment makes Uriel aware of Satan's real identity. It is important also because it is Satan's moment of truth. In the course of the soliloquy he admits that he has done wrong. He admits that God is not a tyrant, that he has made himself fall and seduced his followers without the slightest of excuses. He admits, also, that he cannot repent because he cannot bear to acknowledge anyone as his superior. To be even the highest angel in Heaven is not enough so long as there is a God who is higher. Therefore, his only recourse is to continue to rebel against God, even though he must admit that rebellion is really futile. Thus, in the course of the soliloquy we see Satan knowingly choose evil, knowingly commit himself for all eternity to defying God and to denying his own nature, for since God created him, he is by nature good.

During the course of Book IV Satan assumes other disguises. He observes Adam and Eve in the shape of a cormorant, a bird of prey. He has assumed, then, the shape of something even further beneath himself than a lesser angel. It is, nonetheless, though, a being that can soar into the air. His next disguise is to assume the shapes of the lion and then the tiger in order to get closer to Adam and Eve. In other words, he chooses animals even further from the sphere of reality for which he had been created, since these four-footed animals walk upon the earth. But, again, these are animals that convey some suggestion of nobility. We all think of the lion as the king of beasts, and though tigers are ferocious, they are, to most people's imagination, splendid in their freedom and their power. His next disguise, though, is completely contemptible. He assumes the shape of a toad to be able to whisper into Eve's ear as she sleeps. When he is discovered by Gabriel's lieutenants, he is returned to his own shape, but he has suffered such degeneration that he is unrecognizable. Again, Satan cannot admit how much he has changed. He suffers considerable pain when the fact of his change is forced upon him.

Satan next appears in Book IX. His further degeneration is evident
in his soliloquy at the beginning of that book. He is no longer able
at all to face the truth. The whole speech is made up of laments
of self-pity and irrational shouts against God. The disguise he
chooses in Book IX is that of a serpent. After he has seduced Eve
and, through Eve, Adam, he returns to Hell. Once again, Satan
persuades himself that he will not have to pay for his evil, that he
will be in no way changed by it. But he discovers even more
emphatically than he did at the end of Book IV that he cannot
choose to be a serpent and return with impunity to his original
form. In Book X, just as he is boasting of his achievements to his
fellow devils, both Satan and all the rest of the devils are changed
by God into monstrous serpents. They are forced to assume the
shape Satan once chose to take, and their monstrous appearance
reveals the monsters they have become by choosing to act, not only
against God's will, but against their own natures.

2. Describe the three Hells which Milton distinguishes.

ANSWER: Milton describes three different Hells in *Paradise Lost,*
apart from the Hell of separation from God which links all of them
together. The first Hell is found early in Book I. It is a place of
darkness lit only by flames. The "fiery gulf" into which Satan and
his followers have fallen burns with "liquid fire." The landscape
is volcanic. When Satan gets out of the pool and reaches land, he
finds it "firm brimstone" as hot as the pool. In the distance is a
hill "whose grisly top/ Belched fire and rolling smoke." Marjorie
Nicolson *(Readers' Guide)* thinks Milton based much of his description of this Hell on the Phlegraean Fields, a volcanic region near
Naples. A Jesuit priest, Kircher, who visited Naples in the same
year as Milton (1638) wrote, "You should think yourself almost in
the midst of Hell, where all things appear horrid, sad and lament-
able. . . ."

Pandemonium, described at the end of the first book, is the Second
Hell. Its architect was Mulciber, a fallen angel. Mammon directed
the angelic artisans in their work. Magically the "fabric huge/
Rose like an exhalation" to the sound of sweet music. Miss Nicolson
thinks there may be a reminiscence here of a court masque at
which a "richly adorned palace, seeming all of goldsmiths' work"
came into sight. Even more, Pandemonium recalls St. Peter's
Cathedral in Rome. "The pilasters, architrave, cornices, sculptures,
pillars were all there, though the pillars of St. Peter's are Corinthian,
not Doric, as in Pandemonium. Both the Cathedral and Pandemonium were lighted by 'starry lamps and blazing cressets.' " In both

cases, the building was so huge as to make the living creatures—
men or angels—seem diminished in size.

The fallen angels discover the third Hell after the council breaks up.
They find that the region of Hell is a world of its own, with seas,
rivers, mountains, and valleys. Some parts of it are as cold as
other parts are hot. Some "adventurous bands" explore it and find
"many a dark and dreary vale," many a "region dolorous," fiery
alps, "Rocks, caves, lakes, fens, bogs, dens and shades of death."
Miss Nicolson finds "something of the combined grandeur and
grotesqueness of Kepler's description of the new world in the moon
in these passages. "Milton's frozen wind in Hell is much like
Kepler's. Kepler's lunar mountains, too, tower to vast heights, and
his caverns and fissures on the moon are as profound as Milton's
Serbonian bog. But . . . the important thing is not the source of
the third Hell, but the fact that Milton's Hell is no such limited
and constricted place as Satan and his fallen angels first believed
when they roused from their stupor on the burning lake" (Nicolson, *Guide,* p. 200).

3. What is the effect of the Fall on Adam and Eve?

ANSWER: The specious words of the serpent into Eve's heart "too
early entrance win." The fruit looked delicious, it was noon-time,
and she was hungry. The smell of the fruit aroused her appetite.
So "Forth reaching to the fruit, she pluck'd, she eat." While nature
sighed "That all was lost," and the serpent slunk ·back into the
thicket, Eve immediately felt the effects of the Fall. She eats to
excess as never before.

> Greedily she ingorg'd without restraint,
> And knew not eating Death: Satiate at length
> And height'n'd as with Wine, jocund and boon
> Thus to herself she pleasingly began.

"Greedily," "ingorg'd," "Satiate," "height'n'd," "jocund," and
"boon" all suggest excess in eating and drinking. "Height'n'd as
with Wine," Eve, like a drunken person, is filled with confidence
and high spirits. She praises the tree which gave such fruit, (C. S.
Lewis speaks of her as "worshipping a vegetable" at this point) and
promises to offer it praise every morning. In her over-confidence
she expects to grow more and more mature, the more she eats of
the fruit. She expects to attain "knowledge, as the gods who all
things know." (Note that she says "gods" now, not God.) She
feels that she is reaping the fruits of experience, that Heaven is

too remote to know what she is doing, and that the "great Forbidder" and his spies have other cares. In short, she feels (falsely) that she has got away with disobedience and profitted from it.

The next thing that we notice is her attitude toward Adam. She wonders whether or not she should tell him about her discovery. Both her arguments are selfish. First she thinks she will keep her knowledge secret

> so to add what wants
> In Female Sex, the more to draw his Love,
> And render me more equal, and perhaps,
> A thing not undesirable, sometime
> Superior: for inferior who is free?

So already she is tempted both to deceive Adam and to be (if possible) superior to him, thus upsetting the hierarchy of order. But her next thought is different, though it is equally selfish. Suppose God has seen her disobedience and 'suppose she really dies as a consequence. Could she bear the thought of "Adam wedded to another Eve"? Jealous already in imagination, she decides she could not bear it.

> Confirm'd then I resolve,
> Adam shall share with me in bliss or woe
> So dear I love him, that with him all deaths
> I could endure, without him live no life.

And once more she bows to the tree, committing the sin of idolatry.

Meanwhile, Adam has woven a wreath of flowers for her hair and is looking forward to her return, a little anxious over her welfare. She meets him with a bough of the tree in her hands, and tells him somewhat apologetically that she has missed him. Quickly she plunges into the subject of the tree. The tree, she explains, is not evil or dangerous. It made the serpent wise and Eve wiser than she used to be, "and growing up to Godhead." She wants him to eat it too, for bliss is not true bliss unless it is shared.

> Thus Eve with Count'nance blithe her story told,
> But in her Cheek distemper flushing glow'd.

Adam "Astonied stood and Blank," dropping the wreath he had made. He reproved Eve as "defac'd deflower'd, and now to Death devote." He sees clearly what has happened—Satan has tricked her—but even with his eyes open he knows what he will do: "Certain my resolution is to die." He loves Eve so much that he could not live without her. Even "another Eve" could not make him forget her.

> Flesh of Flesh,
> Bone of my Bone thou art, and from thy state
> Mine never shall be parted, bliss or woe.

He loves her with physical rather than spiritual love, but Eve is delighted that he has offered her so noble a proof of his love. She offers him some of the fruit and he sins quite consciously:

> He scrupl'd not to eat
> Against his better knowledge, nod deceiv'd,
> But fondly overcome with Female charm.

His sin is uxoriousness.

As in the case of Eve, the effect of the sin is immediate. Adam is delighted with the fruit. The two

> . . . swim in mirth, and fancy that they feel
> Divinity within them breeding wings.

Both experience "carnal desire."

> Hee on Eve
> Began to cast lascivious Eyes; she him
> As wantonly repaid; in lust they burn:
> Till Adam thus 'gan Eve to dalliance move

Their mutual attraction now is contrasted with the dignity and beauty of their previous nuptial love. Adam "forbore not glance or toy/ Of amorous intent," and Eve's eyes "darted contagious Fire." On a bank of flowers

> They thir fill of Love and Love's disport
> Took largely of thir mutual guilt the Seal,
> The solace of thir sin, till dewy sleep
> Opress'd them, wearied with thir amorous play.

But their sleep is not light and healthful, as before, but gross and heavy, and when they awake, innocence is gone. Their nakedness,

which previously seemed natural to them, now seems shameful,
and they make themselves loin cloths of fig-leaves. They sit down
to weep, but not only tears, but sinful emotions now appear. "High
Passions, Anger, Hate,/ Mistrust, Suspicion, Discord," now shake
their minds, once visited only by peace,

> For Understanding rul'd not, and the Will
> Heard not her lore, both in subjection now
> To sensual Appetite, who from beneath
> Usurping over sovran Reason claim'd
> Superior sway.

Their mutual recriminations begin. Adam blames Eve for going
off by herself to test her virtue. Eve says first, that Adam would
have been deceived, just as she was, and second, that he should have
stopped her, as she was the weaker of the two. "Is this how you
repay my love?" Adam replies, "I have given up immortal bliss to
stay with you. I warned you about going off alone." So the two
go on bickering, but neither really blames himself. Sin has entered
into the world and into the relationships of men and women. Adam
ate the fruit so as not to be separated from Eve. Ironically, they
are immediately separated by their quarrel.

4. What is the effect of the Fall on Nature?

ANSWER: The sin of Eve and the sin of Adam are both felt in
the world of nature. When Eve swallowed the fruit,

> Earth felt the wound, and Nature from her seat,
> Sighing through all her works gave signs of woe.

Similarly, when Adam ate,

> Earth trembl'd from her entrails, as again
> In pangs, and Nature gave a second groan,
> Sky low'r'd, and muttering thunder, some sad drops
> Wept at completing of the mortal Sin
> Original.

The sun's position is altered so that the earth is affected with
extreme cold and heat. The aspects of the moon and the five
planets is altered so that their effect is evil rather than good. The
winds in their corners "bluster to confound/ Sea, Air, and Shore,"
and the Thunder rolls out its terror. The earth's position in relation

to the sun is changed, so that there are extremes of heat, "else had the spring/ Perpetual smil'd on Earth with vernant Flow'rs."

Moreover, a change in the relationships between beast and beast and beast and man took place.

> Beast now with Beast 'gan war, and Fowl with Fowl,
> And Fish with Fish, to graze the Herb all leaving
> Devour'd each other; nor stood much in awe
> Of Man but fled him.

Adam, mourning "with sad complaint," realized that this was "the end/ Of this new glorious World."

5. What is the significance of the character of Abdiel?

ANSWER: Abdiel appears only in Books V and VI of *Paradise Lost*, but he is, nonetheless, very important. Satan boasts that he is strong enough to stand against authority, strong enough not to bow down to God and the Son. But Satan shows himself over and over again to have been a toady and a hypocrite. He admits that one reason he cannot repent is that if he repents, he will "lose face" before those whom he led to rebellion. Also, Raphael's account of the rebellion in Heaven shows that Satan was a hypocrite. He did not just stand up against God. He flattered God and the Son a whole day before he rebelled against God's edict. And he rebelled only after he had lured his forces away at midnight in an attempt to keep his rebellion secret.

Abdiel, on the other hand, has the qualities that Satan only claims to have. He stands up against Satan at the assembly in which Satan is plotting his rebellion. He cares nothing for the opinion of the rest of Satan's host, and he does nothing at all to disguise his opinions or to flatter Satan. He is openly independent, truly strong. Hence, he is a foil to Satan. It is as though Milton were saying to readers too much impressed with Satan's vaunted independence: "It is not the rebel who boasts and who stands in vain against legitimate authority who is the real hero. The man like Abdiel is the real hero, for he is someone who will stand alone for truth and against falsehood even when all those around him are led into error." Note, furthermore, that Abdiel's independence is manifested in obedience to God, in his acceptance of rightful authority. It is, in fact, his recognition of rightful authority that gives him the vision and the strength to reject Satan's assumed authority.

6. Compare the Unholy Trinity with the Holy Trinity.

ANSWER: According to Christian theology, there are three Persons in the Trinity, God the Father, God the Son, and God the Holy Ghost. In Book II, Milton establishes an unholy Trinity: Satan, Sin, and Death. He bases it on a verse in the Epistle of James (1:15), "Then the lust when it hath conceived, beareth sin; The Sin, when it is full grown, bringeth forth Death." Sin sprang fully grown from the head of Satan, as Athena sprang fully grown from the head of Zeus. Similarly God did not create Christ, the second Person of the Trinity; rather He is said to have been the only begotten Son of God. As God the Father and the Son are of one substance, so Sin and Satan are of the same substance. There is a third Person in the Holy Trinity, the Holy Spirit, who is, according to Christian theology, the love which binds Father and Son together. He is the Spirit through whom the world was created. "And the Spirit of God moved upon the face of the waters" (Genesis 1:2), bringing the creation of the world into being. By contrast, the third person of Satan's trinity is destructive rather than creative. It is Death itself. Death is born of the incestuous relationship of Sin and Satan, a relationship characterized by lust and later by hatred. Death is the bond between Satan and Sin as the Holy Ghost is the bond between the Father and the Son in the Holy Trinity. The Satanic Trinity is held together by hate, as the Holy Trinity is held together by love. Sin and Death are so ugly that at first Satan does not recognize them as his offspring. Sin has changed and has to remind Satan of their previous relationship. Later Death rapes Sin—thus committing incest like his father—begetting the "cry of hell-hounds" who bark unceasingly about the middle of Sin and creep into her womb. Milton is thinking both of Spenser's Error, a monster whose lower half was serpent-like, and of Ovid's account of Scylla, whose lower body was a crowd of howling dogs.

Although he is shocked at their ugliness, Satan sees how he may make use of Sin, for she will open the nine-fold gates and let him out. In return, he will offer both Sin and Death the race of men to prey upon. At this point in the narrative there is another parallel with the Holy Trinity. Sin says (lines 868-70) that Satan will bring her into bliss, "where I shall reign/ At'thy right hand voluptuous, as beseems/ Thy daughter and thy darling without end." Milton's readers would know the Nicene Creed, which said that Christ "sitteth at the right hand of the Father" and would "come again with glory to judge both the quick (i.e., living) and the dead; whose kingdom shall have no end."

After the Fall, Sin (in Book X) grows stronger and reminds Death
that they are inseparable. She proposes that she and Death build a
highway across Chaos to the world where Satan holds power.
Death agrees, saying he can smell his prey on earth ("with delight
he snuff'd the smell/ Of mortal change on Earth." Satan meets his
offspring at the foot of the new bridge. He is pleased with the work
and sends his daughter-wife and son-grandson to rule Earth in his
name. Similarly the Son, the second Person of the Holy Trinity,
goes as God's regent to earth to judge Adam and Eve. He holds out
to the pair the hope of redemption: the seed of Eve (Christ himself)
will crush the serpent (Satan) who brought death into the world.
Christ will achieve the final victory.

7. Is there any hope for Adam and Eve at the end of the poem?
Explain.

ANSWER: "Can He [God] make deathless death?" Can our threat-
ened punishment be averted? This is the question that Adam asks
himself in his agonized soliloquy in Book X. Toward the end of
that book, he and Eve take steps toward their own regeneration.
First Adam recognizes his own responsibility for the wrong he
committed.

> First and last
> On mee, mee only, as the source and spring
> Of all corruption, all the blame lights due.

He is still very angry with Eve, but meanwhile she has been medi-
tating on her own sin and that of Adam. Generously she takes on
herself the blame for both of them, speaking of herself as the
"sole cause . . . of all this woe." Adam is touched by this and his
anger against Eve dies. They vow to support and help each other
"in offices of love." Eve proposes averting the punishment which
is to fall on their offspring either by having no children or by
entering a suicide pact, but Adam decides that they should not
try to avoid the punishment which God's justice meted out to
them and their descendents. He remembers the promise that Eve's
Seed will crush the serpent and sees that suicide would accomplish
nothing. They must hope and trust in God. At the end of the book
both Adam and Eve have learned a new humility. They fall prostrate
before God and "both confess'd/ Humbly their faults."

At the beginning of Book XI the Son tells the Father that the
repentant prayers of Adam and Eve are more pleasing than any

innocence could have offered and promises that by His death He will atone for men's sins, thus mitigating His doom. God sends the archangel Michael to drive the pair out of Paradise. Michael reminds them that they can atone for their sin through their good deeds and that God is present on earth as well as in Paradise. In the vision of the future which Michael now presents to Adam, covering Biblical history to the birth of Christ, he reconciles Adam somewhat to death by showing him that in a fallen world, death is a good rather than an evil, and can be an entry into a new kind of life. When he speaks of Abraham, he says that from his seed shall come a nation in which all men shall be blessed. From his line shall come the deliverer of mankind, the Messiah who will be born of a Virgin and of God Himself. He will defeat Satan by His obedience and by His death. He will rise on the third day, charge His disciples to teach all nations, and ascend into heaven to rule at God's right hand forever.

Adam weeps for joy to hear these tidings and exclaims on God's infinite goodness, which has brought this greater good out of evil. He doesn't know whether to repent his sin or rejoice over it, since it has made possible the coming of Christ, whose life will make possible a higher life for man than would have been possible had man remained in a state of innocence. Thus Milton refers to the paradox of the Fortunate Fall (in Latin, Felix Culpa), which eventually brought Christ into the world and showed men the way to a better life. What this better life is Michael explains. Men can repent and, through obedience and faith, work toward their own regeneration, at peace with God and with themselves. They can find a new "Paradise within," in spite of some sadness and trouble. Eve rejoices:

> Though all by mee is lost,
> Such favour I unworthy am vouchsaf't
> By me the Promis'd Seed shall all restore.

Thus, with a backward glance at Paradise, Adam and Eve, grownups now, fare forth into the world:

> Some natural tears they dropp'd, but wip'd them soon;
> The World was all before them, where to choose
> Thir place of rest, and Providence thir guide:
> They hand in hand with wand'ring steps and slow,
> Through Eden took thir solitary way.

8. The poem sets out to "justify the ways of God to men." How does Milton achieve this end? Consider first the negative justification

which proves that neither Satan's fall nor Adam's is God's fault. Then show all of the ways in which God brings good out of evil.

ANSWER: Milton justifies the ways of God to men negatively when he proves that God is not responsible for the sins of either angels or men. Satan sinned, as the whole action of the poem shows, of his own free will. Not only did he knowingly choose to go counter to God's will in his initial rebellion. He knowingly chooses evil throughout the whole poem, even though he chooses evil at the cost of his own destruction, a destruction that comes about more through his insistence upon doing evil (even though the choice of evil is a choice that goes counter to his own nature), than it does through God's punishment upon him.

God is not responsible for Adam's sin, either. He has made Adam perfect, able to withstand temptation. He has warned Adam that if he eats of the Tree of Knowledge, he will surely die. Furthermore, after God hears of Satan's plan to seduce men, He sends Raphael to warn Adam and Eve again of their need to be obedient to Him. Raphael also warns Adam against his uxoriousness and tells the human pair about the fall of Satan so that they will realize that it is possible to succumb to temptation.

That God is not responsible for evil is not, however, enough. If He is really to win the battle with Satan, He has to bring good out of evil. His first attempt to bring good out of evil comes when He creates the world in answer to Satan's rebellion. The new race of men will fill the places in Heaven the fallen angels have deserted, and their evil will simply be the means which leads God to diffuse His goodness to a whole new order of creation.

When Satan attempts to destroy this new world by seducing Adam and Eve, God retaliates by giving Adam the grace to repent of his sin. He also promises that men will be able, in spite of Satan's malice, to gain Heaven and to join Earth to Heaven in the final judgment. Thus the goodness of God outweighs the evil of Satan. Furthermore, the generosity of the Son in volunteering to assume men's sins in order to save them is far greater than Satan's malice in attempting to destroy them.

God brings good out of evil in other ways, too. The evil of death becomes a good when we realize that in a world distorted by sin death becomes both good and natural. Since men and all other things in God's good world are now subject to corruption, death becomes God's instrument for clearing away the rubble that would otherwise choke the Earth. Also, since men are subject both to old age and to disease, death comes to them as something welcome, as Adam learns from Michael in Book XI.

Perhaps the most convincing way in which God brings good out of evil comes in the development of the characters of Adam and Eve. They are charming children when they first appear in the poem, but they are, nonetheless, children. After they have sinned, and Eve's humility has paved the way for their repentance, they are humbled into a new maturity. They are far more attractive human beings when they leave Paradise than they were during their stay in the Garden. They have learned their limitations, as all human beings since them have learned them, by discovering through bitter experience that they are weak. The discovery gives them the compassion, the charity, and the humility they lacked in the innocence of their days in Paradise.

One subtle way in which the poem shows that good can come out of evil is in Milton's comments on his blindness, in his prayer to light at the beginning of Book III. Milton's blindness is an evil, and he never sees it as anything but an evil. But something good has come out of that evil. Because he is blind, he can fix his attention without distraction upon that inner light, that inspiration, by means of which he can write his poem. He may be shut out from the contemplation of the external world. But he is the freer to contemplate the truths he has learned from Scripture or from God's direct inspiration to him than he would be if he could see.

BIBLIOGRAPHY AND GUIDE
TO FURTHER RESEARCH

MILTON'S BACKGROUND

Hutchinson, F. E., *Milton and the English Mind*, London, 1946.

Bush, Douglas, *English Literature in the Earlier Seventeenth Century*, New York, 1946.

Willey, Basil, *The Seventeenth Century Background*, New York, 1955. These three books are useful introductions to the intellectual and artistic background of the seventeenth century.

MILTON'S LIFE

Darbishire, Helen, ed., *The Early Lives of Milton*, London, 1932. Contains six lives written during the seventeenth and early eighteenth centuries.

Hanford, J. H., *John Milton: Englishman*, New York, 1949.

Tillyard, E. M. W., *Milton*, London, 1930.

Saurat, Denis, *Milton: Man and Thinker*, London, 1925; rev. ed., 1944. Interesting early psychological study of Milton and evaluation of his thought. Much of Saurat's commentary on Milton as a thinker has been questioned. But his insights into Milton's character are still considered vauable.

Belloc, Hilaire, *Milton*, Philadelphia, 1935.

Clark, Donald L., *Milton at St. Paul's School*, New York, 1948. A study which casts light not only upon Milton's youth but also upon secondary education in England during the seventeenth century.

Diekhoff, J. S., ed., *Milton on Himself,* New York, 1939.
This book contains all the personal passages in Milton's works. It should be of considerable interest to anyone doing research on Milton's life.

GENERAL CRITICISM

Note: Many of the biographies of Milton also contain critical evaluations of his works.

Hanford, J. H., *A Milton Handbook,* New York, 1946.
A truly valuable starting point for anyone studying Milton.

Johnson, Samuel, "The Life of Milton" in *Lives of the Poets.* Many editions. This famous work is the starting point for much modern criticism of Milton. Johnson disliked *Lycidas* and disliked Milton, the man, both because of Milton's politics and his Puritanism, but he admired *Paradise Lost* immensely.

Thorpe, James, ed., *Milton Criticism: Selections from Four Centries,* New York, 1950. A collection of critical essays sampling attitudes toward Milton from his day to ours.

Eliot, T. S., *On Poetry and Poets,* London, 1957, pp. 156-183.
These pages present two essays, an early one, in which Eliot attacked Milton, and a later one, in which he modified some of his earlier opinions.

Leavis, F. R., *Revaluation,* New York, 1948.

Adams, Robert, *Ikon: John Milton and the Modern Critics,* Ithaca, New York, 1955.

Smith, Logan Pearsall, *Milton and His Modern Critics,* London, 1940.

Kermode, Frank, ed., *The Living Milton,* London, 1960. The four books just cited present evaluations both sympathetic to Milton and opposed to him.

Daiches, David, *Milton,* London, 1956.

Grierson, H. J. C., *Milton and Wordsworth: Poets and Prophets,* Cambridge, 1949. This is a study of the poetic theories of Milton and Wordsworth.

Tillyard, E. M. W., *The Miltonic Setting: Past and Present*, Cambridge, 1947.

————,*The Metaphysicals and Milton*, London, 1956. A study of Milton's relations to other poets of the early seventeenth century.

Allen, Don Cameron, *The Harmonious Vision: Studies in Milton's Poetry*, Baltimore, 1954. Detailed analyses of Milton's major poems.

MILTON'S VERSIFICATION

Bridges, Robert, *Milton's Prosody*, Oxford University Press, 1921.

Sitwell, Edith, *The Pleasures of Poetry*, London, 1930.

Sprott, S. Ernest, *Milton's Art of Prosody*, Oxford, 1953

MILTON AND MUSIC

Spaeth, Sigmund, *Milton's Knowledge of Music*, Princeton, N.J., 1913.

Brennecke, Ernest, *John Milton the Elder and His Music*, New York, 1934. A study of the achievements of Milton's father in music.

MILTON AND SCIENCE

Svendson, Kester, *Milton and Science*, Cambridge, Mass., 1956.

Curry, Walter Clyde, *Milton's Ontology, Cosmogony, and Physics*, Lexington, Ky., 1957.

Nicolson, Marjorie, "Milton and the Telescope" in *Science and the Imagination*, Ithaca, N.Y., 1956.

Bush, Douglas, *Science and English Poetry*, New York, 1950.

MILTON AND THE CLASSICAL TRADITION

Bush, Douglas, *Classical Influences in Renaissance Literature*, Cambridge, Mass., 1952.

Highet, Gilbert, *The Classical Tradition: Greek and Roman Influences on Western Literature,* New York, 1949.

Osgood, Charles G., *Classical Mythology of Milton's English Poems,* New York, 1925.

INDIVIDUAL WORKS

Note: The student who works on any of the individual poems should, of course, consult the general critical works and the works dealing with special aspects of Milton's poetry. See, especially, Allen, *The Harmonious Vision,* for all of the poems considered here.

COMUS (1634):

Brooks, Cleanth and John Edward Hardy, *Comus* and "Notes on other Readings of *Comus"* in *Poems of Mr. John Milton: The 1645 Edition with Essays in Analysis,* New York, 1951, pp. 187-237. An extremely valuable analysis of the poem. All of the essays in this volume are interesting and stimulating close readings of Milton's early poems.

LYCIDAS (1637):

The student should begin with Samuel Johnson's famous attack on the poem in his *Life of Milton.*

Brooks and Hardy, *Lycidas, op. cit.,* pp. 169-186.

Ruskin, John, "Of King's Treasuries" in *Sesame and Lilies,* Many editions.

Daiches, David, *Lycidas* in *A Study of Literature,* Ithaca, N.Y. 1948.

Patrides, C. A., ed., *"Lycidas": The Tradition and the Poem,* New York, 1961, A collection of critical commentaries on the poem from several periods.

PARADISE LOST

All of the works mentioned as general critical studies of Milton deal with *Paradise Lost.* The following particular studies are of value:

Addison, Joseph. A series of eighteen essays in *The Spectator* papers that did much to establish Milton's reputation in the eighteenth century and to introduce the poems to the audience of the day: the rising middle class. The essays are available in many editions.

Bowra, C. M., *From Virgil to Milton*, London, 1945.
An study of the literary epic and Milton's place in the tradition.

Bush, Douglas, *"Paradise Lost" in Our Time: Some Comments*, New York, 1945.

Ferry, Anne Davidson, *Milton's Epic Voice: The Narrator in "Paradise Lost*," Cambridge: Harvard University Press, 1963.

Lewis, C. S., *A Preface to "Paradise Lost*," London, 1942.
An extremely valuable introduction to the poem for the student.

Peter, John, *A Critique of "Paradise Lost*," New York, 1960.

Stein, Arnold, *Answerable Style: Essays on "Paradise Lost*," Minneapolis, 1953.

Waldock, A. J. A., *"Paradise Lost" and Its Critics*, Cambridge, 1947.

Wilkes, G. A., *The Thesis of "Paradise Lost*," Melbourne: Melbourne University Press, 1962.

Wright, Bernard A., *Milton's "Paradise Lost": A Reassessment of the Poem*, London, 1962.

Brooks and Hardy, "A Note on Reading the Longer Poems," Appendix A of the work cited under *Comus*, pp. 271-281. A brief discussion of Milton's use of language which students should find valuable.

PARADISE REGAINED:

Hughes, Merrit Y., "Introduction" to *Paradise Regained* in *John Milton: Complete Poems and Major Prose*, New York, 1957, pp. 471-482.

Pope, Elizabeth M. *"Paradise Regained": The Tradition and the Poem*, Baltimore, 1947.

Stein, Arnold, *Heroic Knowledge: An Interpretation of "Paradise Regained" and "Samson Agonistes,"* Minneapolis, 1957.

Tillyard, E. M. W., "The Christ of *Paradise Regained* and the Renaissance Heroic Tradition" in *Studies in Milton,* London, 1951.

SAMSON AGONISTES:

Bowra, C. M., *Samson Agonistes* in *Inspiration and Poetry.* London, 1955.

Krouse, F. Michael, *Milton's Samson and the Christian Tradition,* Princeton, N.J., 1949.

Parker, William R., *Milton's Debt to Greek Tragedy in "Samson Agonistes,"* Baltimore, 1937.

Stein, Arnold, *Op. cit.,* under *Paradise Regained.*

Note: All of the works listed under Milton and the Classical Tradition will probably have material on *Samson Agonistes.*

GENERAL WORK

Bush, Douglas, ed., *The Complete Poetical Works of John Milton,* Boston: Houghton, Mifflin Co., 1915.

Nicolson, Marjorie Hope, *John Milton: A Reader's Guide to His Poetry,* London: Thames and Hudson, 1964.

Robins, Harry F., *If This Be Heresy: A Study of Milton and Origen,* Illinois Studies in Language and Literature 51, Urbana: University of Illinois Press, 1963.

Sensabaugh, George F., *Milton in Early America,* Princeton: Princeton University Press, 1964.

Smart, John S., ed., *The Sonnets of Milton,* Glasgow: Macklehose, Jackson and Co., 1921.

NOTES

NOTES

NOTES

NOTES

MONARCH® *NOTES* AND STUDY *GUIDES*

ARE AVAILABLE AT RETAIL STORES EVERYWHERE

In the event your local bookseller
cannot provide you with other
Monarch titles you want —

ORDER ON THE FORM BELOW:

Complete order form appears
on inside front & back covers
for your convenience.

Simply send retail price, local
sales tax, if any, plus 35¢ per
book to cover mailing and
handling.

TITLE #	AUTHOR & TITLE (exactly as shown on title listing)	PRICE
	PLUS ADDITIONAL 35¢ PER BOOK FOR POSTAGE	
	GRAND TOTAL	$

MONARCH® **PRESS, a Simon & Schuster Division of Gulf & Western Corporation**
Mail Service Department, 1230 Avenue of the Americas, New York, N.Y. 10020

I enclose $ .... to cover retail price, local sales tax, plus mailing
and handling.

Name _____
(Please print)
Address _____

City _____ State _____ Zip _____

Please send check or money order. We cannot be responsible for cash.